The Art of Maurice Sendak

Selma G. Lanes The Art of

Maurice Sendak

Abradale Press/ Harry N. Abrams, Inc.

Cover: from Where the Wild Things Are. *1963. Pen-and-ink line and watercolor. 9 x 19³⁄₄"*

Title page: from the animated film Really Rosie, *starring the* Nutshell Kids. *1975. Pencil and tempera. 10¹⁄₄ x 38¹⁄₈"*

Table of Contents: from Lullabies and Night Songs. *1965. Pen-and-ink line and watercolor. 1¹⁄₈ x 7¹⁄₄"*

Endpapers: act curtain design for the opera version of Where the Wild Things Are. *1979. Pen-and-ink line and watercolor. Approx. 7 x 9³⁄₄"*

Photography for this book was done by Will Brown, John Gruen, Paulus Leeser, and Gordon Smith

Editor: Robert Morton
Designer: Gilda Kuhlman
Associate Editor: Patricia Gilchrest

Library of Congress Cataloging in Publication Data

Lanes, Selma G.
    The art of Maurice Sendak.

    Includes index.
    1. Sendak, Maurice. 2. Illustrators—United
States—Biography.   I.   Title.
NC975.5.S44L36   1984   741.64′2′0924   84-6370
ISBN 0-8109-8063-0

Illustrations © 1980 Maurice Sendak
Text © 1980 Selma G. Lanes

Printed and bound in Japan

TABLE OF CONTENTS

Introductory Note   7

Brooklyn Beginnings   9

Out the Window   29

The Long Apprenticeship   47

A Controversial Triumph   77
Where the Wild Things Are

The Art of the Picture Book   109

Inspired Pastiches   127
Work of the Sixties

Jennie   151
The Love of My Life

In The Night Kitchen   173
A Picture Book "From the Direct Middle of Me"

Grimm Purpose   191

Branching Out, Digging Deep   209

Recurring Themes   237

Portrait of the Artist as A Private Person   251

A Chronology of Books   271

Index   273

Introductory Note

There is no better-known illustrator of children's books in our time than Maurice Sendak. Since the publication in 1963 of his most popular picture book, *Where the Wild Things Are,* which he both wrote and illustrated, his work has been almost as much in demand in France, Germany, Great Britain, Japan, and the Scandinavian countries as it is here in the United States. Sendak is credited by many critics, educators, and knowledgeable readers of children's books with being the first artist to deal openly with the feelings of young children. His receipt in 1970 of the international Hans Christian Andersen Medal, the closest approximation to a Nobel Prize in the world of children's books, for the body of his illustration gave official confirmation to what his admirers already knew: that his pictures had made and were continuing to make a major contribution to the literature of childhood. The artist has said of his work, "If I have an unusual gift, it's not that I draw particularly better or write particularly better than other people—I've never fooled myself about that. Rather, it's that I remember things other people don't recall: the sounds and feelings and images—the emotional quality—of particular moments in childhood."

What Sendak's early life was like, then—who his parents were, where he grew up, what happened to him, and, most of all, how he reacted to the people, places, and events of his childhood—is of more than routine biographical interest.

Ultimately, however, it is the artist's work that speaks most eloquently of his childhood, as it does of the illustrators he has admired and emulated, and the places, objects, and beings that have moved him deeply. This picture biography covers the work—both published and heretofore unpublished—of Sendak's career thus far. It is the first major retrospective of the most important children's book illustrator of our time.

S. G. L.

Opposite: from the memorial volume, Randall Jarrell 1914–1965. *1967. Pen-and-ink line.* 5¹³/₁₆ x 3¹³/₁₆"

Maurice Sendak '78

Brooklyn Beginnings

The dominant figures of his childhood were two—"Mickey Mouse and my severe and bearded maternal grandfather." Maurice Sendak never actually knew his maternal grandfather, except from a faded large photograph that haunts him to this day. A surprisingly wistful-looking Old World patriarch, he had died in Europe years before his grandson's birth. "As a child," Sendak remembers, "I assumed he was the exact image of God." Mickey Mouse, on the other hand, was entirely of this world and to be seen everywhere in the 1930s. The young Maurice, like countless other children from coast to coast, chewed Mickey Mouse gum, brushed his teeth with a Mickey Mouse toothbrush, played with Mickey in a seemingly endless variety of games, and read about his adventures in all shapes and sizes of comic strips and storybooks. "Best of all," Sendak says, "was seeing him on the movie screen. In the darkened theater, the sudden flash of his brilliant, wild, joyful face—radiating great golden beams—filled me with an intoxicating unalloyed pleasure." Years later, the artist would use an adaptation of this image on both the half title and final page of his picture book *In the Night Kitchen,* to communicate the triumphal joy of his own hero named Mickey.

Maurice Sendak was born on June 10, 1928—the same year as Walt Disney's illustrious mouse—"in a land called Brooklyn," as he once put it; "a regular tree-

lined ghetto separated by a river from the most magic of all lands, New York City, that fantastic place rarely visited but much dreamed of." He was the third and youngest child of Sarah and Philip Sendak, both immigrants who had come to New York before the First World War from small Jewish *shtetls* outside Warsaw. The family name Sendak means "sponsor" or "godfather" in Hebrew. Maurice's brother Jack was five when Maurice was born, his sister Natalie nine.

As a child, he was called Murray, and his earliest color drawing—of Mickey Mouse done when he was six—is formally signed "Murray Sendak." Looking on Disney's mouse hero as "an early best friend," Sendak has often used their common first initial for the names of the heroes in his own books: Martin of *Very Far Away,* Max of *Where the Wild Things Are,* and Mickey's own name for the sunny protagonist of *In the Night Kitchen.*

Philip Sendak, the romantic son of a comparatively well-to-do merchant (he sold lumber as well as owned a general store), had crossed the Atlantic in pursuit of a free-spirited, cheerful girl with whom he was in love. But by the time he arrived in America, she was already married to someone else.

Sendak's mother, the eldest daughter of a poor Talmudic scholar who supported his family by running a grocery and dry-goods store, was sent to America by her family when her much-beloved father died at the age of forty. Though

Above left: Sendak's paternal grandparents. Above right: the artist's maternal grandfather. Opposite: Sarah Sendak with Jack, infant Maurice, and Natalie. 1928

10

Sarah was scarcely fifteen at the time, the plan was that she would work and earn enough to bring her mother, brothers, and sisters to the United States. It was a pattern followed by many immigrant families too poor to leave their homelands as a unit.

Perhaps what drew Philip to Sarah was the similarity of their Old World backgrounds, or a shared sense of the loss of someone loved, or the fact that Sarah had curly auburn hair and loved to dance. In any event, he married her about two years after his arrival. They honeymooned in the Catskills, where another immigrant friend had opened a small hotel called Charlie's.

It was at Charlie's that the family spent two weeks every summer during Sendak's boyhood. And it was at Charlie's that the twelve-year-old Sendak and another young guest, Pearl Karchawer, exchanged World's Fair rings. The friendship was short-lived, because Pearl died unexpectedly less than a year afterward, during surgery for a congenital back defect. It was Sendak's first experience of the death of a contemporary, and one that affected him deeply. He would include Pearl Karchawer in the dedication to his best early book, *The Sign on Rosie's Door*:

> Remembering Pearl Karchawer
> all the Rosies
> and Brooklyn

Some of Sendak's happiest memories are of his father: "During my childhood, which seemed like one long series of illnesses, he invented beautiful imaginative tales to tell to me and my brother and sister. He was a marvelous improviser and would often extend a story for several nights." Sendak feels that these stories constituted the first important source from which his work developed. One tale that he remembers vividly was about a child taking a walk with his parents. "Somehow he becomes separated from them, and snow begins to fall. The child shivers in the cold and huddles under a tree, sobbing in terror. Then, an enormous, angelic figure hovers over him and says, as he draws the boy up, 'I am Abraham, your father.' His fear gone, the child looks up and also sees Sarah. When his mother and father find him, he is dead." Angels were active participants in most of Philip's stories, and Sendak attributes his fondness for them to his father. Indeed, he remembers his father's telling him once when he was sick that if he stared hard enough out the window he might see an angel flying by. If he did, it was a sign of good luck and he would get better quickly. "But, if you blink, you'll miss it," his father told him. After Philip left the room, the boy stared as hard as he could for minutes at a time. Suddenly, he thought he saw an angel. He screamed for his father, "I saw it, I saw it!" And Sendak remembers his father's pleasure when he rushed back into the room. "He was as thrilled as I was."

Looking back on the story of the dead boy with Abraham and Sarah, the artist views the tale as partly based on the power of Abraham in the Jewish tradition: "The father who was always there—a reassuring father, even when he was Death. But the story also reveals how tremendously my own father missed his parents. Not all his tales were sad, though. Often, he would tell us his own versions of Old Testament stories. My father could be very witty, even if his humor was always on the darker side of irony."

Whatever the nature and sources of Philip Sendak's narrative gift, it made a lasting impression on his sons. They, too, had their father's flair for storytelling. As young boys, both Jack and Maurice wrote, illustrated, and bound their own storybooks. Often the brothers combined cut-out newspaper photographs or comic-strip segments with original drawings of members of the Sendak family.

When Maurice was six years old, he and the eleven-year-old Jack collaborated on a flamboyant narrative called *They Were Inseparable*. It was about a brother and sister who, in Sendak's words, "had a hankering for each other. It was a naive and funny book. We both idolized our sister; she was the eldest and by far the prettiest child, and we thought she was the crown jewel of the family. So, because we adored her, we made the book about a brother and a sister. And at the very end of the story, as I recall, there is an accident: the brother is in the hospital, and they don't think he's going to recover. The sister comes rushing in, and the two of them just grab each other—like the conclusion of *Tosca*—and exclaim '*We are inseparable!*' Everybody tries to pull them apart, but they jump out the window of the Brooklyn Jewish Hospital together. Yes, you see, we *did* know dimly that there was something wrong and it had to end badly."

"I imagine that all siblings have such feelings," Maurice once mused to Jonathan Cott in an interview for *Rolling Stone* magazine. "The learning process makes children aware that these feelings are taboo, but before they learn that, they do what comes naturally. My parents weren't well-to-do, and we had only two beds—my brother and I slept in one, my sister Natalie in the other. And often we'd all sleep together in the same bed—because Natalie was terrified of bedbugs. My parents would come into the room—sometimes with an uncle and aunt—and my mother would say: 'Look, see how much they like each other.' We didn't know that this could be that, and that this . . . kids only find that out later."

If Natalie was the prettiest sibling, Maurice was easily the frailest. The most

Overleaf: this detail of a drawing from Fly by Night *(page 217) relates to the family photograph on page 11. 1976. Pen-and-ink line*

13

dramatic and dangerous of Sendak's early illnesses was measles, which he contracted at age two and a half. He was sick for thirteen weeks—since double pneumonia rapidly followed—and it left him with a well-earned reputation for being delicate. "I remember being terrified of death as a child," says Sendak. "I think a lot of children are, but I was scared because I heard talk of it all around me. There was always the possibility I might have died of the measles or its aftermath. Certainly my parents were afraid I wouldn't survive. Once, later on, when I asked for a sled, my father said, 'You, a sled? You'll have pneumonia in a week.'"

"I was a miserable kid," Sendak confides. "I couldn't make friends. I couldn't skate great, I couldn't play stoopball terrific. I stayed home and drew pictures. You *know* what they all thought of me: sissy Maurice Sendak. Whenever I wanted to go out and do something, my father would say, 'You'll catch a cold.' And I did. I did whatever he told me."

Whatever the fears of his family, Sendak early developed a talent for observing and savoring, rather than actively participating in, the life around him. He clearly recalls during the convalescence from another of his serious illnesses—scarlet fever—at the age of four, "I was sitting on my grandmother's lap, and I remember the feeling of pleasant drowsiness. It was winter. We sat in front of a window, and my grandmother pulled the shade up and down to amuse me. Every time the shade went up, I was thrilled by the sudden reappearance of the backyard, the falling snow, and my brother and sister constructing a sooty snowman. Down came the shade—I waited. Up went the shade—the children had moved, the snowman had grown eyes. I don't remember a single sound." As if watching a silent movie, Sendak was enthralled by each slight shift in scene from one real-life frame to the next. As a young man, he would sit by himself at another apartment window and sketch the children outside, recording passing moments of play on the street below. Again the window served as a front-row seat on the mini-dramas of childhood taking place outside. From the time he was very young, Sendak remembers being conscious of gathering usable material for books. "I used to examine my grandmother all the time," he says, "and place her in various fantasies. And I was so aware of the streets on which I lived that, even now, I remember them in complete detail—how many houses there were, who lived in which one, what the people looked like."

Recently, to emphasize a point about the artist's need to detach himself from daily events, Sendak spoke of the French writer Jules Renard, author of *Poil de Carotte*, a poignant novel of childhood. He cited the following extract from Renard's published journal: "The beauties of literature. I lose a cow. I write about her death, and this brings me in enough to buy another cow." With characteristic Gallic matter-of-factness, he neglected to mention that he was also keeping the memory of the animal alive. "That's the wonderful thing about being an artist," Sendak said admiringly. "You can use the material of your life over and over, and always make of it something new. In that way, it's never dead for you." Certainly this was the case in 1966 when he wrote *Higglety Pigglety Pop!* in an effort to immortalize his beloved Sealyham, Jennie. In much the same spirit, two years later, when his parents were in failing health, he wrote *In the Night Kitchen*—dedicated to them.

Though Sendak now jokes about his tender constitution as a boy, there is little doubt that his early illnesses colored his attitude and approach to life. Consider the heroes of his own first books: Kenny of *Kenny's Window* is an introverted daydreamer, and Martin in *Very Far Away* is a fussy, passive loner.

In public statements—his 1970 acceptance speech on receiving the Illustrator's Medal of the Hans Christian Andersen Awards, for one—Sendak usually characterizes his childhood as happy: "All in all, what with loving parents and sister and brother, a deeply satisfying childhood." But he was perhaps more candid and revealing when he tried to convey to Virginia Haviland, the head of the children's book division of the Library of Congress, the power and charm that Charles Dickens's work holds for him. "On one level, Dickens is telling you a straightforward story. But underneath, there is the intensity of a little boy staring out at everything and looking, and examining, and watching, and feeling deeply, and suffering immensely, which is what I think makes Dickens a superb writer." This same sort of intensity is what makes Sendak so rewarding an artist, but the quality seldom springs from a happy, cloudless childhood.

Sendak has often spoken of "the boredom and loneliness" of children, particularly the tedium of long summer days in the city, imprisoned on a single block. "We were never allowed to cross the street, walk in the gutter, or, on pain of death, come upstairs except at mealtimes, or to go to the bathroom, or to stop profuse bleeding. Snacks and other necessities were dropped out the window, and street fights were screechingly arbitrated by mamas in adjacent windows."

Sendak's father was a dressmaker, one of three partners in Lucky Stitching, a shop on Thirty-fourth Street in Manhattan, and before his younger son's birth, the business was apparently a thriving one. Early family snapshots show the artist's sister Natalie dressed in velvet, and his brother Jack outfitted in a black Little Lord Fauntleroy suit. "But then I was born in 1928," says Sendak, "and my father lost every cent he had. You only see us in *shmattas* [Yiddish for rags] from then on." Though they managed to survive the Depression years as

"a good, lower-middle-class family," the fall in the Sendaks' fortunes after Maurice's birth possibly served to increase parental anxiety over the frailty of their youngest offspring. There is no question that he was pampered and overprotected. When Sendak was grown up and called home twice a week from Manhattan, his mother would shout to his father, "Your darling's on the telephone!"

Sendak has characterized his mother, always called Sadie, as "a withdrawn, scrimping woman. She was never stingy toward her own family or relations," he hastens to add, "but she was always worried. She also had a gruff, abrupt manner, because I think that any display of feeling embarrassed her." Apparently her way of showing affection was to rush into her children's bedroom and shout "Whoooot!" thereby scaring her youngest child out of his wits. "I'd be lying in bed and I'd yell, 'Why'd you do that?!' I'd be angry with her, and she'd be hurt.

Or she would come in and start tickling my feet. Now I'm very ticklish and I couldn't stand it. I'd scream until she stopped. It was her constant pain not to understand why I didn't realize she was being affectionate." Sendak remembers with some feeling a parting he and his mother had at a hospital elevator a few weeks before her death in 1968. "She kissed me," he says incredulously, as if overcome by the directness of her expression of love.

Given his fevers and indispositions, and the family concern about his delicate constitution, the young Maurice spent a great deal of time indoors, much of it in the kitchen with his mother. The cozy sense of warmth and intimacy emanating from his illustrations for *In the Night Kitchen* doubtless owes much to this period of his life. His mother would be cutting dough or preparing soup, and the small boy reveled in the different, wondrous smells.

When he was six or seven, Maurice was allowed to accompany his parents to the movies on Friday nights, so that Sadie could get the weekly dish being given away by the local theater to encourage neighborhood patronage. "I loved the whole experience—going to a movie with my parents on a Friday night, and then, at the end, bleary-eyed, falling out of the theater into the dark streets of the city. It was almost too exciting."

Sendak's earliest memories of places, of movies, and even of books tend to be earthy and sensual, rather than cerebral. He remembers clearly the first real book he received as a child: *The Prince and the Pauper*, a birthday gift from his sister when he was nine. A getting-acquainted ritual, which he recalls in detail, began with that book.

The first thing I did was to set it up on the table and stare at it for a long time. Not because I was impressed with Mark Twain; it was just a beautiful object. Then came the smelling of it. I think the smelling of books began with *The Prince and the Pauper*, because it was printed on particularly fine paper, unlike the Disney Big Little Books I had gotten previously, which were printed on very poor paper and smelled poor. [Not that this lessened his enjoyment of such favorites as *Mickey Mouse, Detective; Mickey Mouse, Airmail Pilot;* and—best of all—*Mickey Mouse in Pygmyland.*] *The Prince and the Pauper* not only smelled good, but it also had a shiny, laminated cover. I flipped over that. And it was solid—I mean, it was bound very tightly. I remember trying to bite it, which I don't imagine was what my sister had in mind when she bought the book for me. The last thing I did was to read it. It was all right. But I think my passion for books and bookmaking started then.

Early in life, Sendak knew he wanted to be an illustrator, to be involved with books in some way—"to make books and to touch books—there's so much more to a book than just the reading of it," he says. "I've seen children fondling books, and that's all the reason in the world why their books should be beautifully produced."

He has told friends that books seemed alive to him as a child, as did many other juvenile objects he was fond of. All children have intense feelings about certain dolls or other toys, but in Sendak's case this kind of relationship was heightened because, up to the age of six, he spent so much time in bed being sick. Alone for much of the day, he developed friendships with objects. To this day, he keeps near him certain toys he played with when young.

As a child, Sendak neither went to museums nor saw art books. "I was really quite rough, artistically," he says. "*Fantasia* was probably the most aesthetic experience of my childhood, and that's pretty dubious as an example." There were the ubiquitous comic books, Walt Disney, and—more important than these—radio and the movies, especially the movies. Thirties films like Busby Berkeley's *Gold Digger* series, *King Kong* and other monster films, and the Laurel and Hardy comedies supplied the raw stuff that his picture books are made of.

On those memorable occasions when their older sister, Natalie, took Maurice and Jack to the movies, they went not to the neighborhood theater but to Radio City Music Hall, or to the Roxy, in Manhattan, "that fantastic place rarely visited but much dreamed of." Maurice saw *Snow White* and, later, *Pinocchio* in Manhattan. "Now the point of going to New York was that you *ate* in New York," Sendak explains with obvious relish. "Somehow to me New York represented eating. And eating in a very fashionable, elegant, superlatively mysterious place like Longchamps." As a child he found the very names Longchamps and Schrafft's wondrously exotic. "You got dressed up, and you went uptown, and it was night when you got there, with lots of windows lit and signs blinking. Then you went straight to a place to eat. It was one of the most exciting things of my childhood," Sendak says, "to cross the Manhattan Bridge on the BMT and see the city approaching, to get there and have your dinner, then go to a movie and come home."

As for other forms of recreation, on weekends the entire family would sometimes take the subway to visit relatives in different parts of Brooklyn. (The elder Sendaks never owned a car.) Maurice looked forward particularly to the outings to Brownsville, where an uncle owned a candy store. As he looks back on these visits now, they all seem to have revolved around food and eating. His mother would spend a good part of Friday preparing special dishes to take.

Opposite: Brooklyn rooftops, a background painting for the animated film Really Rosie, *starring the Nutshell Kids. 1974. Pencil and tempera. 9 x 21"*

Never much of a success as a student, Sendak disliked school from the moment he entered his first-grade classroom, where he screamed because he missed his mother. "I hate, loathe, and despise schools," he says. "The only part of my childhood that was truly punishing and suffering was school." To this day, he tends to look on all formal education as the sworn enemy of the imagination and its free, creative play. "Perhaps it's a rationalization," he admits, "because I hated it so much, but school is bad for you if you have any talent. You should be cultivating that talent in your own particular way." He still remembers the heavy-hearted feeling of waking on school mornings and reluctantly forcing himself into motion. "In order to get there, I had to talk myself out of a state of panic nearly every day. I couldn't stand being cloistered with other children—I never did like competition—and I was usually so embarrassed that I stammered." The stammer sometimes recurs at times when he is ill at ease or upset. Almost the only in-school activity he enjoyed was reading books from the school library on his own; *Pinocchio in Africa* and *Toby Tyler* were early favorites.

To Sadie Sendak the artist owes the curiously peripatetic quality of his childhood. The family never lived in any one place for more than a few years, always moving just a step ahead of the painters. "Every third year, my sister, my brother, and I acquired a new apartment, street, school, and neighborhood," Sendak remembers. "My mother loathed the chaos and stink created by house painters, and in those faraway, dim days, they *did* paint every third year." If domestic life had to be disrupted, Sadie preferred a total change of scene. And so the family wandered from one Bensonhurst neighborhood in Brooklyn to another. Only once did they live in a big apartment house. Generally they occupied a four- or six-family structure, no more than three or four stories high. All of these had stoops which served as gathering places for kids on the block. Sendak, in fact, tends to recall his childhood in neat, apartmentalized segments, identified by various Brooklyn addresses. It was on Sixty-ninth Street, for example, when Sendak was seven or eight, that he had as his best friend a girl named Tzippi. "Her sister Rosie had had polio," Sendak remembers, "and was the first Rosie in my life. I once wrote a long, unpublished story about Tzippi." Another reason that Sendak has fond memories of this address is that it coincided with a period of robust good health—a rarity in his early childhood. "I won't ever forget that street where I used to play outdoors a lot with my brother. As it turned out, I was healthier than anyone gave me credit for being." Sendak, in fact, was seldom sick again, aside from catching whatever colds and mild communicable diseases other kids routinely got.

Another upbeat address was 1717 West Sixth Street. "That was the happiest of our little excursions," he says. "We lived there from the time I was nine until I was twelve. I was overweight—fat, really. But my best friend, Heshie, was even fatter. That's when my sister took me to see *Snow White and the Seven Dwarfs.*" It was a time, too, when Sendak saved money to buy Disney coloring books and discovered one of his "expertise things." He could tell film stories that held the neighborhood kids spellbound. His special favorites were *Mystery of the Wax Museum*, *The Phantom of the Opera*, and *Devil-Doll*. The first is about a Dracula-style hero who lures victims into his house and then drops them into a vat of boiling wax; and the last, starring Lionel Barrymore, is about a Fagin-like villain who reduces a group of ordinary mortals to miniature size and forces them to pursue a life of crime. Sendak was very happy at 1717 West Sixth.

The next address the family moved to, on West Fourth Street, turned out to be as disastrous as 1717 was good. Though the new apartment was just a couple of blocks from where they had been living, Sendak never again saw Heshie—or his other friends, Alvin, Nini, and Phyllis. "I might just as well have crossed the Atlantic Ocean," he says. "I went to a different school and I lost them all."

In 1941 Sendak was bar-mitzvahed from the new address. The United States had already entered the Second World War, and he remembers that on the morning of his bar mitzvah his father received a letter from Europe informing him that his own father was dead. Philip also had brothers and sisters and their families in Poland, and was in the process of trying to bring them to this country. None would survive the Holocaust.

Meanwhile, Natalie had become engaged to a Brooklyn boy whom both brothers liked very much. When the young man was drafted, he and Natalie made plans to marry, but he was shipped overseas unexpectedly, and there wasn't time. Less than a year later, Natalie received a call from her fiancé's family informing her that he had been killed in action. For months afterward, Natalie was inconsolable. Maurice, too, was deeply affected by this death and by its effect on his sister. Jack had recently been drafted, and the family's anxiety about his safety increased. When the family learned that Jack had been sent to the Pacific, the tension in the apartment was almost unbearable. West Fourth Street was the place the Sendaks waited out the war.

By this time, Sendak was at Lafayette High School, where he remained an indifferent scholar except for art classes. Here, he had an easygoing teacher who provided his students with interesting setups to draw and paint, but left them pretty much alone otherwise. Sendak blossomed under this benign regime and was considered one of the three most talented artists in the school. He contributed work to both the yearbook and the literary magazine. For the school paper

he created a comic strip called *Pinky Carrd* about life in the classroom. Now that he was a serious art student, he began to visit the Museum of Modern Art and the Metropolitan Museum of Art. Degas, Chagall, and Matisse were Sendak's favorite painters, and the influence of the German graphic artist Kaethe Köllwitz can be easily discerned in many of his illustrations during this period.

In the summer of 1943, as much to ward off the boredom of the long vacation as to teach himself something about illustration, Sendak wrote the story and did the pictures for a book version of Prokofiev's *Peter and the Wolf,* a piece of music he adored at the time. In the next long holiday period, he worked on his own illustrated adaptation of Oscar Wilde's story "The Happy Prince." The year after, he drew pictures for a more congenial American work, Bret Harte's *The Luck of Roaring Camp,* copying out the text of this tale about a group of rough-and-tumble miners who take on the care of a baby. Later, he produced a set of pictures to accompany the libretto of Charpentier's opera *Louise,* designing, as he had done before, a book complete with binding, endpapers, and full-color illustrations. These were his first projects on his own, without Jack's collaboration.

After school, Sendak had a job with All-American Comics, where he filled in background details for the *Mutt and Jeff* strip. (The war enabled many art students to find jobs that would otherwise have been unavailable to them.) He added houses and trees where necessary and provided puffs of dust to indicate a running figure's speed. Something of a celebrity at Lafayette, he was interviewed by one of the school newspaper's reporters in 1945, his senior year. Described as

Above: Sendak's comic strip for his high school newspaper, The Lafayette News. *1944. Pen-and-ink line. 10³⁄₄ x 3". Opposite: Sendak's earliest published book illustrations, for the physics textbook* Atomics for the Millions. *1947. Pen-and-ink line. Left: 4¹⁄₄ x 4³⁄₄". Right: 2¹⁄₂ x 4³⁄₄"*

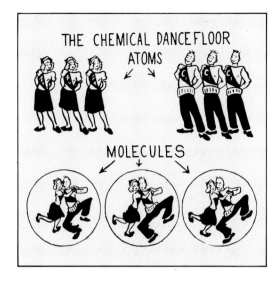

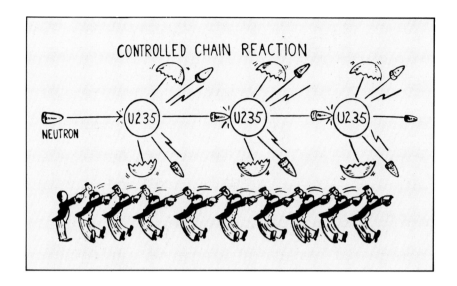

"mild-mannered Maurice," he was pressed for his views on various matters related to his métier. Among other things, Sendak said: "Art must advance as rapidly as music; it shouldn't remain static. Artists must try to get away from realism, because photography can give us all the accuracy and detail we want. Instead, we should drift toward expressionism, where personal feelings and pure emotion are put to work. Artists must have more originality, see beyond what is apparent." Of his hero at the time, the creator of Mickey Mouse, he went on to say, "Walt Disney is the greatest exponent of a new form of art [animation] which will leave a permanent imprint on civilization." Certainly so far as expressing personal feelings and pure emotion in his work went, Sendak was to be remarkably faithful to these early views. And though he would modify his opinion of Disney as he grew in sophistication and graphic skill, he has never lost his interest in, or admiration for, Disney's pioneering courage as an animator.

The element of Jewishness in Sendak's character and work has complex implications and should not be overlooked or underestimated. Though both parents and children went to synagogue on the High Holy Days, the family was certainly not particularly religious. Yet Sendak remembers throwing up the first time he ate lobster (forbidden by Jewish dietary laws) at the urging of one of Natalie's more worldly beaus. He himself has spoken of his "American childhood composed of disparate elements strangely concocted, a childhood colored with the memories—never lived by me—of *shtetl* life in Europe, vividly conveyed to me by my immigrant parents—a conglomerate fantasy life typical perhaps of many first-generation children in America. It was composed, on the one hand, of feeling as though I lived in the Old Country—the fabulous village world of my parents—and, on the other, of being bombarded with the full intoxicating gush of America in that convulsed decade called the thirties. . . . Simply, childhood for me was *shtetl* life in Brooklyn, full of Old World reverberations—and Walt Disney, and the occasional trip to the incredibly windowed 'uptown' that was New York—America!"

From his parents, Sendak got dramatically contrasting pictures of life in Poland. His mother told frightening stories of Cossacks descending on the Jewish town of her childhood, and of being hidden with her brothers and sisters in the dark cellar of her father's store. The artist's father, on the other hand, spoke of ice-skating on a lovely pond and the small pleasures of a comfortable middle-class life. In part, their attitudes may have stemmed from their own personalities and what each chose to remember, but they also reflected to some degree the consequences of being poor in contrast with being well-off.

When Sendak was awarded the international Hans Christian Andersen Medal, the first American illustrator to be so honored, he jokingly suggested that, in his case, its name should be altered to the Hans Jewish Andersen Medal. And though he has long since left the insularity of his early life behind, he retains an outsider's apartness from the world at large. There remains the sense of separateness that colored his feelings as a small boy from a sheltered Jewish community in Brooklyn, crossing the river into "the incredibly windowed" cosmopolitanism of Manhattan. Considering the young Sendak's fondness for windows as a means of sharing in the activities of those more robust and free than himself, his choice of adjective is particularly telling.

When Sendak first began to illustrate books, several reviewers commented, usually with vague uneasiness, on Sendak's portrayal of children who were "too European"—probably a reflection of his perception of Brooklyn as a kind of all-American *shtetl*. "They were just Brooklyn kids," Sendak says, "old before their time. Many of them resemble the kids I grew up with. Most of them were Jewish, and they may well look like little greenhorns just off the boat. They had—some of them, anyway—a kind of bowed look, as if the burdens of the world were on their shoulders."

Others have observed that most of Sendak's children bear a marked resemblance to the artist himself. He agrees. "Yes, they're all a kind of caricature of me. They look as if they've been hit on the head and hit so hard they weren't ever going to grow any more." In the early days of his career, Sendak was often asked why his children were so drab. "Well, they may be drab," he once replied, "but they're not innocent of experience. Too many parents and too many writers of children's books don't respect the fact that kids know and suffer a great deal. My children show a lot of pleasure, but often they look defenseless, too. Being defenseless is a primary element of childhood. And often, I am trying to draw the way children feel—or, rather, the way I imagine they feel. It's the way I *know* I felt as a child. And all I have to go on is what I know—not only about my childhood then, but about the child I was as he exists now."

Here Sendak pauses, for he is about to attempt an explanation of one of his most cherished private beliefs. "You see, I don't really believe that the kid I was has grown up into me. He still exists somewhere, in the most graphic, plastic, physical way for me. I have a tremendous concern for, and interest in, him. I try to communicate with him all the time. One of my worst fears is losing contact. The pleasures I get as an adult are heightened by the fact that I experience them as a child at the same time," he says. "Like, when autumn comes, I as an adult welcome the departure of the heat, but simultaneously, as a child would, I start to anticipate the snow and the first day it will be possible to use a sled. This dual apperception does break down occasionally—usually when my work is going badly. I'll get a sour feeling about books in general, and my own in particular. The next stage is annoyance at my dependence on this dual apperception, and I reject it. Then I get really depressed. When excitement about what I'm working on returns, so does the child. We're on happy terms again." Being in this kind of touch with his childhood is vital to Sendak, but it doesn't make him certain that he knows what he's doing in his work. "Especially in books for children under six," he says, "I don't think anyone really knows what kids that young like and don't like. They're fluid creatures—like moving water. You can't stop one of them at any given point and know exactly what's going on."

It was the Swedish film director Ingmar Bergman who once told a newspaper interviewer, "My films are my interior studios, and these studios were shaped when I was a child. All of us collect fortunes when we are children—a fortune of colors, of lights and darkness, of movements, of tensions. Some of us have the fantastic chance to go back to this fortune when grown up." Certainly this has been Sendak's happy fate as an artist.

"I have an endless fascination and absorption with childhood," Sendak has told many interviewers through the years, "an obsession with my own childhood." It is an absorption that has put countless thousands of adults in closer touch with their own childhoods and continues to enrich the fantasy lives of young readers and listeners the world over.

Out the Window

Although Sendak had had little in the way of formal art training when he graduated from Lafayette High School in 1946, he was not eager to go on to art school. He considered himself lucky to land a first full-time job working in the warehouse of Timely Service, a Manhattan window-display company. Here he helped to build models for store windows, occasionally getting an assignment as congenial as constructing out of chicken wire overlaid with papier-mâché life-size figures of Snow White and the Seven Dwarfs, which were then painted.

Sendak loved the work. "It was one of the best times in my life. I was in Manhattan, I was meeting all kinds of people I'd never met in Brooklyn. They were people who felt they were really artists and considered their work for Timely Service as just a job that enabled them to paint seriously at night." One of the artists Sendak met at Timely was the painter Russell Hoban, who later became a children's book author and illustrator. Russell, who was married, often invited his younger colleague home to his apartment for dinner. "He and his wife Lillian and I became good friends," Sendak says. Once, when the couple had a serious argument and Russell moved out of the apartment, Hoban and Sendak rented a bright first-floor studio on Tenth Avenue near Forty-ninth Street. They even got a dog named Trixie, whom they promptly renamed Garance after the heroine of

Opposite: Rosie's house (detail), from a Brooklyn sketchbook. 1950. Pencil and watercolor. 8⅛ x 5¼" Above: from A Hole Is to Dig. *1952. Pen-and-ink line. 1⅛" x 1⁷⁄₁₆"*

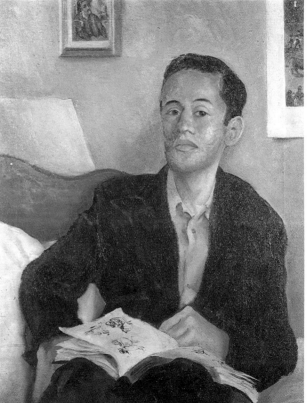

Izzie. 1949. Oil on hardboard. 20 x 16". Mama. *1949.*
Pastel. 24 x 18". Jack. *1949. Oil on canvas. 28 x 22"*

Papa. *1949. Charcoal. 24 x 18″. Natalie. 1949. Charcoal.
24 x 18″. Jack. 1949. Conte crayon. 24 x 18″*

the French film *Children of Paradise*. She turned out to bear an inexplicable grudge against nuns. Whenever a window was left open and anyone in black habit passed by, Garance leaped to the fray. Since the studio was near a Catholic school, her idiosyncrasy proved troublesome.

Sendak loved the feeling of being on his own in New York, a sensation that was destined to be short-lived. Within three months, Russell and Lillian were back together, and Maurice was forced to give up the studio because he couldn't afford the rent. For another brief period, Sendak shared quarters in Manhattan, this time with an old Brooklyn friend, Izzy Fiedler, who was working as a fabric designer in New York. The location, over a bar in the East Fifties, wasn't conducive to concentration or a good night's sleep, for that matter, and once again, Sendak moved back to his parents' apartment in Brooklyn.

After almost two years on the warehouse crew at Timely, Sendak got what was considered a major promotion. He was moved into the department that created the window displays which were constructed in the warehouse. But he wasn't

happy with the change. The department consisted mostly of older people, and so, when some of his younger friends were fired, in the summer of 1948, Sendak left. "Out of a job, out of sorts, and out of money, and—worse—having to live at home with my parents again," as he remembers this bleak period, the artist turned seriously to sketching "out my window" for distraction and solace. He still cherishes a tattered homemade sketchbook titled "Brooklyn Kids, Aug. 1948," which is, in its way, a landmark Sendak document. Among other quick sketches of neighborhood children—one is titled "Allen the Urinator"; another is accompanied by a snatch of dialogue: "Keep your hands off my brother!"—it contains the artist's earliest pictures of Rosie, the child who looms so large in his imaginative development as an illustrator and author. "It seems," Sendak reminisced years later, "on the evidence of that sketchbook and the ones that came quickly after, that the better part of my day was spent at the window Rosie-watching." The books are indeed crammed with drawings of Rosie, her family and friends, and—along the margins of the pages—frantically jotted bits of precious Rosie monologue. One of

Left: self-portrait. 1945. Oil on canvas board. 24 x 17¾". Right: self-portrait with towel headdress. 1949. Pastel. 24 x 18"

the last pencil drawings, captioned "Easter Sunday, April 1949," depicts a somewhat subdued Rosie awkwardly decked out in her church-going finery.

Those early, imprecise, wavery sketches, Sendak feels, "were filled with a happy vitality and joy that was nowhere else in my life at the time." They also form the first rough delineation of the child on whom all his future heroes and heroines would be modeled.

During that same jobless summer, Maurice and his brother Jack—recently discharged from the Army—worked together constructing six ingenious wooden mechanical toys modeled after eighteenth-century German lever-operated toys. Sendak cannot remember where he and Jack might have seen such toys at that time of their lives, except in a scene from the Disney film *Pinocchio*—in Geppetto's workshop, where the old cobbler looks over the collection of animated wooden toys he has made in his spare time. The Sendak brothers' toys, mounted on rectangular stands no more than six inches long, were painstakingly engineered to enact dramatic high points from "Little Miss Muffet," "Little Red Riding Hood," "Hansel and Gretel," "Aladdin's Lamp," "Old Mother Hubbard," and "Pinocchio." Jack masterminded all the movable parts, while Maurice helped with the carving and did the painting of the figures and their settings. The brothers even enlisted the aid of Natalie, who, in the evenings after she came home from work, made the wolf's blanket for "Little Red Riding Hood" as well as bits of finery for other toy scenes. It was almost as if the trio were engaged in a last-ditch effort to recapture their childhoods. (Maurice was twenty at the time.) When the brothers enthusiastically took their prototypes to F. A. O. Schwarz, the big Fifth Avenue toy store, their work was respectfully examined, even admired, but they were told that their wooden toys would be too expensive to produce in large enough quantities to make a profit. "Nor were we ready to compromise if a compromise had been suggested," Sendak says. "We visualized a workshop full of little old men creating the wooden parts, and we would not have permitted any kind of plastic substitute." It was about this time, the artist remembers, that his father got fed up with having two grown sons sitting around the house playing with toys and shooed them out into the world of adult responsibility.

At F. A. O. Schwarz, the window-display director, Richard Nell, had been sufficiently impressed with the way in which Maurice had designed and painted the toys to offer him a job as an assistant in the construction of the store's window displays. Sendak gladly accepted. For the next three years, while working in the toy store during the day, he supplemented his education by attending evening classes in oil painting, life drawing, and composition at the Art Students League. Despite his general antipathy to school, Sendak feels that he learned a great deal from his instructor in composition, John Groth. An accomplished illustrator in black-and-white, with what Sendak characterizes as "a busy line derived from Daumier, his favorite graphic artist," Groth was the illustrator of dozens of adult books, often ones produced in expensive limited editions. "He was important for me," the artist says, "because he communicated a sense of the enormous potential for motion, for aliveness in illustration. And because he himself was so deeply committed to the field, he was able to convey how much fun creating in it could be."

F. A. O. Schwarz itself, which had an excellent children's book department at the time, provided an education of sorts in the varieties of children's book illustration. For the first time in his life, Sendak was exposed to the work of great nineteenth-century illustrators like George Cruikshank, Walter Crane, and Randolph Caldecott. He also saw and was enormously impressed by the graphic work of many of the new postwar European illustrators—the Swiss artists Hans Fischer, Felix Hoffmann, and Alois Carigiet—whose books were brought to this country by Margaret McElderry, then children's book editor at Harcourt, Brace and World.

By 1950, Sendak had become friendly with the Schwarz book buyer, Frances Chrystie. When Miss Chrystie found out about the young artist's interest in children's-book illustration, she offered to introduce him to Ursula Nordstrom, children's-book editor at Harper and Brothers (the publishing house whose books Sendak happened to admire most). It was somehow arranged that Miss Nordstrom would simply drop by the store's studio on a day in the spring. Sendak happened to have a broad sampling of his little pictures tacked up on the walls. As reticent in her way as the artist was in his, Miss Nordstrom looked intently at the work and said little; but, never one to hesitate in the presence of talent, she called Sendak the next day and offered him the chance to illustrate a collection of tales, *The Wonderful Farm* by Marcel Aymé. He immediately accepted. "It made me an official person in children's books," Sendak says. It was also the beginning of a professional and personal relationship that nurtured and shaped Sendak's entire career in children's books.

Of the artist at that time, Miss Nordstrom recalls, "He was very young when I met him. Very shy. I asked him how old he was, and he said twenty-two-and-a-half. He didn't project his personality at all." As for his first impression of the illustrious Harper editor, then in her mid-thirties, Sendak says, "I loved her on first meeting. My happiest memories, in fact, are of my earliest career, when Ursula was my confidante and best friend. She really became my home and the person I trusted most. Those beginning years revolved around my trips to the old Harper offices

Overleaf: mechanical toys. 1948. Wood, string, paint. Top: "Aladdin's Lamp." Base height: 5⅞". Bottom: "Little Red Riding Hood." Base height: 1". Page 37: "Little Red Riding Hood." 1980. Pen-and-ink line and tempera. 10⅝ x 11⅜". Pop-up paper engineering by Intervisual Communications, Inc.

on Thirty-third Street and being fed books by Ursula, as well as encouraged with every drawing I did. We had our disagreements, but she treated me like a hot-house flower, watered me for ten years, and hand-picked the works that were to become my permanent backlist and bread-and-butter support. Ursula is not only an enormously gifted editor; she's generous of herself with young people and makes an incredible personal investment in their careers." It was through Ursula Nordstrom that Sendak was taken to every important book gathering as a Harper illustrator and was introduced to librarians and booksellers all over the country.

Recalling those early years, Miss Nordstrom says, "I had never met anyone like him before. He could imitate people wonderfully well, from the person who sat across from him in the subway to various celebrities. He had a marvelous Mamie Eisenhower routine. He would come into the Harper offices a great deal and was briefly even a manuscript reader. For a while, he was interested in a young woman in the office, and though she irked me by never getting to work on time, I was careful not to be too hard on her. I thought then she might be the future Mrs. Sendak.

"He was wonderful to work with, too," says his Harper editor. "You had only to raise a question about one of his manuscripts, and he was quick to see when a line wasn't right. If there were times when I was unsure of something he felt strongly about, I always knew I could trust his instincts. He's moody and temperamental," Miss Nordstrom grants, "but less so than a lot of small talents I've known. My God, he's a genius, and I can imagine no greater joy than that I've had working with him over the years and watching him develop."

Actually, Aymé's *Wonderful Farm* was not Sendak's first appearance as a published illustrator. In his senior year in high school, thanks to the interest and generosity of a fatherly Lafayette physics teacher, Hyman Ruchlis, Sendak had received his first professional illustrating commission—doing a number of spot drawings in black-and-white for a postwar physics textbook, *Atomics for the Millions*. Remembering how desperate he was at that time for both encouragement and the opportunity to begin somewhere in the world of books, Sendak is still deeply appreciative of this problem-fraught maiden assignment, for which he received $100. Never much of a science student, the neophyte illustrator struggled valiantly to keep his approach lighthearted and, at the same time, accurate. One of his happier attempts was a mildly frenetic drawing entitled "The Chemical Dance Floor," which featured three chlorine atoms (Cl = boys), taking as partners three jaunty sodium atoms (Na = girls), thereby forming a lively trio of dancing salt molecules ($NaCl$).

In addition, the same year Sendak received the Aymé assignment, he illus-

Opposite: mechanical toys. 1948. Wood, string, paint. Top left: "Old Mother Hubbard." Base height: 1³/₁₆". Top right: "Hansel and Gretel." Base height: 1¼". Bottom left: "Little Miss Muffett." Base height: 1". Bottom right: "Pinocchio." Base height: 1⅝"

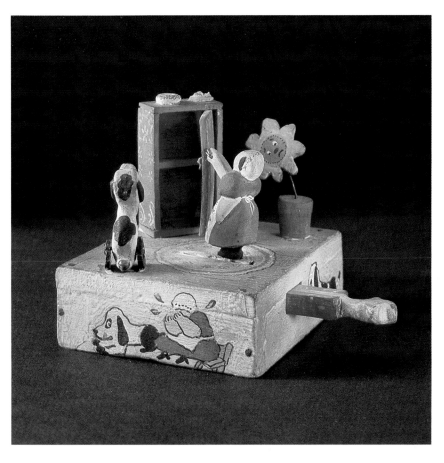 

trated Robert Garvey's *Good Shabbos, Everybody*, a simple story about the Sabbath, for the United Synagogue Commission on Jewish Education. He got the job through the recommendation of the well-established children's book artist Leonard Weisgard, who was serving as the commission's art adviser on a series of picture books about the Jewish holidays. (Sendak had met Weisgard while working at F. A. O. Schwarz.) Even in these earnest and awkward first illustrations, done in three colors, the young artist exhibits an almost uncanny ability to make palpable the emotional reality of the text, the warm family atmosphere in which its characters exist and act, and the psychological sparks of life which bind them together. There is already in the gestures and expressions of the grandparents and small children—as well as in the cozy, claustrophobic aura of Jewish family solidarity Sendak so clearly projects—a preview of what would become Sendak's forte: the gift for getting beneath the surface of things and revealing truths previously considered beyond the province or propriety of young children's books.

Once over the elation of having been entrusted with the Aymé work, his first children's book assignment for a major publisher, Sendak remembers being "scared stiff." In Groth's composition course, the artist had studied the graphic work of Goya, Daumier, and Doré, and he decided to give his black-and-white illustrations for the Harper book a traditional fairy-tale look, based in equal parts on lessons learned from Doré and from the Cruikshank-illustrated books he had examined in Schwarz's book department. There are remarkably accomplished single drawings of animals—particularly one of a fox eyeing a bantam cock hungrily, and another of a trio of foxes—that foreshadow his masterly black-and-white drawings for his Grimm collection, *The Juniper Tree*. And there is a full-page illustration, late in the tale, of two little girls dancing that might well have come directly from the artist's "out-my-window" Brooklyn sketchbooks. Although *The Wonderful Farm* with Sendak's illustrations received generally favorable notices when it appeared in 1951, it made no special impact on the book world.

While on vacation in South Carolina, Sendak completed illustrations for a second Harper book—Ruth Sawyer's *Maggie Rose: Her Birthday Christmas*. On his return, Ursula Nordstrom asked if she might leaf through his sketchbooks. It was on the strength of his 1948–49 illustrations of Brooklyn children playing in the street—running, jumping, standing still, fighting, talking, moping—that she offered him the book that was, soon after its publication, to make him a major figure among children's book illustrators: Ruth Krauss's *A Hole Is to Dig*.

An early example of what later came to be called "concept books," this modest Krauss text was, in 1952, an anomaly. It had no plot. Instead, by talking

Opposite: painted metal tray. 1953. Oil on tin. Diameter: 15¾"

with, and listening closely to, children, the author assembled a series of genuine children's definitions, among which were "Dogs are to kiss people," "Hands are to hold," and "The world is so you have something to stand on." Before he began his illustrations, Sendak was given the opportunity to look through a batch of definitions that editor and author had already eliminated. One—"Buttons are to keep people warm"—was reinstated by the young illustrator and inspired one of his most appealing drawings. Though the general idea has since been imitated widely, no other book has had the freshness or brash charm of *A Hole Is to Dig*, much of the credit being due to the energetic, lovingly observed little people of Sendak's rendition. They, in turn, owe almost everything to the artist's apprenticeship "out my window." Whether they are wiggling their toes, being licked by their dogs, or slogging through the mud on a rainy day, Sendak's earnest "little greenhorns" are heartbreakingly childlike, never sentimentalized or patronized.

How Sendak came to be selected as the book's illustrator is one of those happy accidents that biographers delight in. The well-known children's-book artist Nicolas Mordvinoff (winner of the Caldecott Medal in 1951) was offered the assignment first, but had turned it down. He felt that there was no book to be made from—and certainly no coherent illustrations possible for—so fragmentary and elusive a text. As soon as Sendak read the script, on the other hand, he was unqualifiedly enthusiastic. "He exploded with pleasure and won over a skeptical Ruth Krauss immediately," Ursula Nordstrom remembers. "It was like being part of a revolution," Sendak says. "This was the first time in modern children's-book history that a work had come more or less directly from kids." The notion was so startling to academics, apparently, that *A Hole Is to Dig* was adopted for use in a Columbia University course on the creative use of language.

Sendak still speaks with gratitude of the many lessons he learned from Ruth Krauss while working on that first close collaboration, as well as on other of her fifties books. "In the beginning, I spent many weekends in Connecticut with Ruth and her husband Crockett Johnson [the newspaper cartoonist and creator of the popular comic strip *Barnaby*]. Ruth was an experienced children's-book author and a wonderfully patient teacher. She was my school. I'd say that almost eighty percent of the layout ideas for *A Hole Is to Dig* came from her. [The suggestion for the small format was Johnson's, since he had a predilection for small characters and small books.] It's unimaginable not to have worked with Ruth as closely as I did." The artist, understandably, is very much against the current publishing practice of keeping authors and illustrators apart. "It's insane," he insists. "I mean, someone writes a book and takes certain months or years to do it. The book then goes to a publisher, and someone else illustrates it without the poor writer's being able to say a word. There is no reason why collaboration should not be encouraged. There would have been no *A Hole Is to Dig*—or any other of my Krauss books—without that close association with Ruth herself."

A Hole Is to Dig was innovative in other ways. Its format was smaller than the conventional child's book, and the artist was forced to direct more than casual attention to the importance of page design. Its success brought back what Sendak calls "the little-book vogue." The work was printed on brown-tinted paper, and, to enhance its old-fashioned look, Sendak deliberately incorporated a good deal of ink crosshatching, in the tradition of mid-nineteenth-century English and German illustrations, into his pen-and-ink drawings. Ruth Krauss had generously agreed to share the book's royalty with the young artist. Otherwise, Sendak might well have been offered a flat fee only, as many an illustrator still is for a first picture book.

Critical reception of the work was gratifyingly enthusiastic. "A unique book," proclaimed the *New York Times*. "Entirely original in approach," said the *Horn Book Magazine*, the leading independent publication devoted to children's books. "The illustrations are perfect." So well received was the book in its first year that Sendak at last felt confident enough to give up his full-time job at F. A. O. Schwarz and to leave his parents' house as well. (Though *A Hole Is to Dig* did not sell spectacularly well in the early years following its publication, the demand for it has been steady. As it neared its thirtieth birthday, the book was still selling more than three thousand hardcover copies a year.) The artist moved into his own small apartment on Greenwich Street, the first of several Village addresses. He had become—wonder of wonders—a free-lance illustrator!

Ready cash was in short supply at the outset. For a while, during 1953, Sendak tried to augment his income by decorating trays with pictures of his already familiar children at play. He abandoned this impractical money-making scheme when it took him three months to finish the first tray. Fortunately, however, assignments from Harper came with gratifying steadiness—seldom the case with newcomers. Though Sendak willingly allowed Ursula Nordstrom to monopolize his graphic talent during the next several years, there were flattering signs of interest from a number of other major publishers. In 1955, the artist illustrated a second holiday book for the United Synagogue Commission on Jewish Education, *Happy Hanukah, Everybody*. Much more sophisticated as an illustrator by this time, he provided the tale with two thoroughly individualized principal characters, Joel and Mimmy, who owe much to his "out-my-window" sketchbook. The same year, reluctant to turn down any assignment that paid and might broaden his experience, the artist

provided spot drawings in black-and-white for a collection of seven cautionary tales, *Little Stories on Big Subjects*, for the Anti-Defamation League of B'nai B'rith—minor work, but also unmistakably indebted to his "out-my-window" period.

Much of Sendak's illustration in these first professional years reveals a rare ability to depict both the very old and the very young with genuine sympathy untinged by false sentiment. Whatever the artist still lacked in draftsmanship or polish at this stage in his career was compensated for by the close observation and depth of feeling his drawings almost always reveal. Increasingly, too, his books bear witness to an illustrator becoming more adept at using the confines of the printed page to serve his own graphic purposes. In his two-color illustrations for Ruth Krauss's *A Very Special House*, for example, the small-boy protagonist opens the work by facing the reader and beginning to dance. He then conducts a skipping, jumping, constantly-in-motion tour of the magical house he would like to live in. At the story's end, his back to the reader, the same small boy walks nonchalantly off stage—turning his head slightly to smile over his shoulder, as if bidding his audience a fond farewell. Clearly Sendak already sensed that the picture book was to be his stage, one adaptable to an ever expanding repertoire. More and more, his illustrated pages spring to life. Ruth Krauss's *I'll Be You and You Be Me*—a book about friendship and fantasizing and love ("Love is they could push you down in the grass and it doesn't even hurt")—is chock-full of lively one- and two-page mini-dramas; Beatrice de Regnier's *What Can You Do with a Shoe?* is a nonsensical catalog of unlikely uses for footwear, furniture, headgear, and crockery. Its sprightly pictures make highly effective use of a crisp black line, giving an edge to otherwise soft red-and-gray-wash illustrations. In Sendak's black-and-white drawings for longer works as well—Meindert DeJong's *Shadrach*, *Hurry Home, Candy*, and *The Wheel on the School*—there are other harbingers of the more versatile artist to come: suggestions of the lyrical landscapes that will enrich his later work; signs of branching out both into a freer style (combining a soft wash with his ink line) and into other locales—Holland, for one—with convincing ease. Each new book bears irrefutable evidence of an artist rapidly moving beyond the confines of the view from his Brooklyn window into a broader realm of visual sophistication and life experience.

The Long Apprenticeship

The Work of Others

Opposite: the "Giant Snorrasper," from Schoolmaster Whackwell's Wonderful Sons. *1962. Pen-and-ink line, with two wash separations. 9¼ x 5⅞". Note: the artist altered the format of this drawing to fit this page. Above: from* The House of Sixty Fathers. *1956. Pen-and-ink line. 3¼ x 3½"*

To view Sendak's career as an illustrator from its beginnings is to be moved by his painstaking mastery of style, of several styles—of any style, in fact, that happened to serve the work at hand. From his earliest books on, the artist always rated interpretive illustrations, pictures that expand a given text and add a new richness of meaning to it, above both narrative illustration, which simply mirrors the author's words, and mere graphic decoration. "To be an illustrator is to be a participant," he says, "someone who has something equally important to offer as the writer of the book—occasionally something more important—but is certainly never the writer's echo." If looking out the window and sketching what he saw represented Sendak's first art school, then learning selectively from other illustrators' work constituted a self-styled graduate-study program. "I discovered those artists from all over the world who seemed to speak directly to me," he has said, "and, as a young man trying to discover myself, I leaned heavily on those sympathetic friends."

But Sendak has never been a mere copyist or acquirer of surface mannerisms. Whatever he took from the artists he admired he turned to his own ends. His career is, in many ways, a marvelously frugal one. Every lesson he has ever learned, either from the work of others or from his own struggles with particular manuscripts he illustrated, has been made use of again and again. With each reappear-

47

ance, the lesson undergoes some transformation by which it gains in both intensity and graphic power. Sendak's rise to the pinnacle of children's book illustration has been no accident. The artist spent the fifties and early sixties consciously expanding his graphic repertoire by emulating the work of master illustrators, both present and past. Always a lover and collector of books, he made a deliberate effort to track down works mentioned by Miss Nordstrom, Ruth Krauss, or other illustrators and friends. In the early 1950s, Sendak greatly admired the work of the Russian-born Nicolas Mordvinoff. He still finds Mordvinoff's illustrations for *The Two Reds* full of graphic invention and a near-perfect picture book. When the artist came to illustrate Beatrice de Regnier's *The Giant Story*, a work he completed before *A Hole Is to Dig*, though it was published afterward, he consciously tried to draw as boldly as Mordvinoff.

To follow Sendak's development through the years is also to become aware of how much of a piece his art is, whatever outside influences may have been incorporated into it at a given moment. In the drawings for his first Harper book, Aymé's *The Wonderful Farm*, are clearly recognizable precursors of the animals which appear in his later books as much surer, more pointed characterizations. Other early illustrations exhibit glimmers of the composition, feeling, and content of the highly polished pictures done at the height of his career. In Aymé's *The Magic Pictures*, for example, there is an illustration of a child mounted on a wolf's back that is strikingly similar in look and spirit to the drawing he provided some twenty years later for the tale "The Golden Bird" in *The Juniper Tree*.

Occasionally, an idea or character from one of the books he has illustrated will work its way into the artist's imagination and be stored for future use. The definition from Ruth Krauss's *A Hole Is to Dig*—"A mountain is to go to the top / A mountain is to go to the bottom"—almost certainly provided the inspiration for *The Christmas Mystery*, a puzzle that Sendak created two decades later for the December 1971 issue of *Family Circle* magazine. Here Sendak's small hero and heroine are observed scaling a mountain peak, then slipping and sliding down the other side. (In the end, the mountain turns out to be Santa Claus—a purely Sendakian flight of fancy.) And surely the flying-boy figure in a Ruth Krauss book of 1956, *I Want to Paint My Bathroom Blue*, is a recognizable antecedent of the airborne young hero of Randall Jarrell's *Fly by Night*. The figure also resembles three of Sendak's own heroes: Kenny, of *Kenny's Window*; Max, of *Where the Wild Things Are*; and Mickey, as he flies through the starry sky in *In the Night Kitchen*. The full-color pictures in *I Want to Paint My Bathroom Blue* also have that easy, almost musical flow that is characteristic of Sendak's own picture books. By the mid-fifties, some readily identifiable hallmarks have become established in the

Opposite: from I Want to Paint My Bathroom Blue. *1956. Pencil and watercolor. 8¼ x 13⅝"*

artist's work: notably, spunky, round-faced little heroes and know-it-all small heroines who can play through any script with grace and aplomb. There are also a number of supporting players who begin to reappear from book to book. One is the Sendak lion. In Ruth Krauss's *A Very Special House*, for example, a simple, linear version of the king of the beasts makes its bow. It reappears, soggy-legged but riveting, in illustrations for Jack Sendak's story *Circus Girl*, in *The Nutshell Library*'s *Pierre*, in *Hector Protector*, and, most memorably, in his major prose work, *Higglety Pigglety Pop!* The lion scarcely changes from work to work. His forelegs look like nothing so much as those of a well-stuffed lion suit. But despite—or possibly because of—the curious contours, Sendak's beast is electrifying in each of his appearances. The persistence of lions in the artist's work may well bear some dim relation to the number of MGM movies he saw from the age of six. Sendak himself says he was afraid of dogs as a small boy, and the lion may well represent that fear. Lions, of course, have been known to eat people and are classic symbols of aggression.

During the fifties and early sixties, Sendak did occasional illustrations for book jackets: for five collections of Ogden Nash's verse and for a paperback edition of George Eliot's *The Mill on the Floss*. He also provided artwork for various advertisements and did story boards for several animated cartoon sequences on Jell-O Instant Puddings derived from his two-color drawings for *A Very Special House*. Whatever jobs came his way during this period resulted from his growing reputation as a children's book illustrator. (Sendak has never had an agent for his work.) Certainly his seven collaborations in ten years with the Dutch-born author Meindert DeJong reflect the gradual broadening and deepening of his graphic powers. The realistic demands made by each of DeJong's stories, set as they are in various foreign locales which were unfamiliar to the artist, required that Sendak do careful graphic research. For the most part, this was undertaken at the picture collection of the New York Public Library. As early as *Shadrach* (1953), the first of the DeJong books, Sendak's black-and-white illustrations appear to be under some liberating influence: the line is freer and bolder than ever before. The artist's black-wash-and-line drawings for their second joint effort, *The Wheel on the School*, are also more relaxed than his earliest published illustrations. Yet, though Sendak's figures, both here and in *Shadrach*, are in Dutch dress, they still bear a distinct resemblance to the artist's mildly melancholy little Brooklyn children. So delighted was DeJong with Sendak's pictures for his books that he dedicated *The Singing Hill*, their last collaboration, "To Maurice Sendak, who illuminates my things, because we are a pair." It is in this book that one of the artist's most evocative early illustrations appears: that of a boy looking out a window. The scene is invested with feeling—with longing, loneliness, and a sense of apartness from the world.

The artist made a first trip to Europe in 1953 and found that the experience held him in good stead when he came to do the artwork for Aymé's *The Magic Pictures*. "This book gave me the perfect chance," he said when it was done, "to exploit my feelings for southern France—not to make direct replicas of the wonderful little towns, but to attempt to get that vital, hearty, wry quality into the little girls, Delphine and Marinette. I wanted them to stand for all that France meant to me, as little as I saw of it that first time abroad." He did manage to spend time in Paris, much of it at the Louvre, where the richness of the collection surpassed anything he'd imagined. "There they all were, the real thing—Titians, Da Vincis, Raphaels!—paintings I had always read about and maybe even seen reproduced, but there they were right in front of me."

His early popularity notwithstanding, Sendak has at no time during his career been in step with the mainstream of American children's book illustration. In the mid-fifties, when bold exploitation of color, abstract design, outsized formats, and showy technical virtuosity abounded, Sendak's work remained consistently low-key, curiously retrograde and nineteenth-century in spirit. The use of crosshatching was introduced into his illustrations right from the start—in *The Wonderful Farm*. The technique was developed by wood-engravers in the eighteenth and nineteenth centuries; by crossing two or more sets of parallel lines, an artist could indicate modeling and achieve a sense of three-dimensionality. Crosshatching is brilliantly exploited in Else Holmelund Minarik's *Little Bear* books; Sendak's drawings actually achieve the look of nineteenth-century wood engravings. From the work he did during the late fifties, Sendak emerged as a conscientious and respectful student of the past, an innovator in the sense that he was unafraid to follow his own bent and incorporate earlier influences into his pictures. While other American illustrators like Paul Rand and Leo Lionni were adapting the brash visual techniques of the advertising age to children's books, and the French artist André Francois was bringing the wit and sophistication of adult cartoons, posters, and magazine covers to simple stories for the very young, Sendak was, as he himself sums up these years, "borrowing styles and techniques shamelessly, trying to forge them into a personal language. I was an arranger more than an innovator."

At various times, to different audiences, Sendak has provided long and changing lists of those artists—mostly of the nineteenth century—who have deeply marked his work. The credits have ranged from the English mystic William Blake, whom the artist regards as "the chief head influence on my art," to the elegant turn-of-the-century French illustrator Louis Maurice Boutet de Monvel; from Thomas Rowlandson and George Cruikshank, with their virtuoso

draftsmanship and good-natured caricatures of English life, to the German comic artists Heinrich Hoffmann and Wilhelm Busch; from such Victorian illustrators as England's Randolph Caldecott, Walter Crane, Arthur Hughes, and Samuel Palmer to the early twentieth-century American comic-strip artist Winsor McCay. The artist has also been influenced by the Italian artist Attilio Mussino, who provided the varied and energetic illustrations for Collodi's *Pinocchio* (1880). Of the eclectic Mussino, Sendak says admiringly, "My eyes were opened by the offhand virtuosity of the man, the ease with which he commanded a variety of styles, controlled them all, blending them and still managing to keep them subservient to the tale. He taught me respect for finish and style, as well as a certain disregard for these qualities. Style counted, I now saw, only insofar as it conveyed the inner meaning of the text being illustrated."

All through the 1950s and early sixties, Sendak not only studied the work of those nineteenth-century English and German illustrators he admired, he also began to collect first editions of their work and, when possible, original art. He owns a number of Caldecott watercolors; three paintings and other graphic work of the mystical English artist Samuel Palmer; an original hand-colored engraving by William Blake; and a number of first editions of works illustrated by Blake.

In reviewing Sendak's early illustrations, an interested observer cannot fail to see the work coming into sharp, sure focus between 1955 and 1962. The more certain touch is dramatically evident in such childlike works as Ruth Krauss's *Charlotte and the White Horse*, Sendak's first book in full colors and one much influenced by his fondness for Blake and Chagall. (The color in all his earlier books had been achieved by the use of separate overlays done on acetate, with the colors selected from available printer's inks and applied at press time. By contrast, the artist working in full color simply paints using whatever colors he chooses, and the artwork is reproduced by a sophisticated process which separates the various colors for printing.) Sendak's growing mastery is also present in the first of the bear-family quintet of easy readers, *Little Bear*. This book, which marked the beginning of the artist's second highly successful collaboration with a seasoned author, testifies eloquently to his infatuation with the great English and German illustrators of the nineteenth century. His Victorian drawings for *Little Bear* display a depth of sympathy for Minarik's characters—particularly for the warm relationship between Little Bear and Mother Bear—that virtually guaranteed the tale's success. Sendak gives another reason for choosing a Victorian setting for *Little Bear*. "Of course I wanted Mother Bear to be an image of warmth and strength—nothing less than motherhood itself. So I dressed her in Victorian costume, because those voluminous skirts, the voluminous sleeves, and her voluminous figure all made for the

Opposite: from Charlotte and the White Horse. *1955. Pen-and-ink line and watercolor. 4 x 3⅞"*

53

strong and comforting tenderness I wanted her to exude. And when Little Bear
sat in her lap, I had her envelop him. The folds of her skirt surrounded him.
There couldn't be a safer place in all the world than Mother Bear's lap." The
Minarik text is composed of four tender domestic vignettes: it is cold outside and
Mother Bear makes a snowsuit for Little Bear to wear; Little Bear improvises a
birthday soup when he thinks Mother Bear has forgotten his birthday; Little Bear
takes a trip to the moon, and Mother Bear joins in the make-believe; Mother Bear
grants Little Bear's wish for a bedtime story, and he, in turn, complies with a wish
of hers. So at home was Sendak in the world of nineteenth-century illustration that
much of his best work, from Sesyle Joslin's *What Do You Say, Dear?* to George
MacDonald's *The Light Princess*, has this period as its setting.

Sendak's illustrations for the *Little Bear* readers (books written and designed
so that children can read them by themselves by the end of first grade) provide
persuasive evidence of the high seriousness the artist brings to his craft. In the first
book of the series, which he looks back on as "a perfect book," Sendak struggled
to make the gestures of the bears true to their ursine natures as well as to recognizable human actions. He had great difficulty with one scene, in which Mother
Bear must sweep a floor. His first sketches were awkward and unconvincing. Finally, he posed a human model sweeping, slowly transforming the sketch into
Mother Bear believably performing the same task. By the time the third book,
Little Bear's Friend, was published in 1960, Mother Bear has grown perceptibly
softer and more tender in appearance. Her costume, too, is more lovingly individ-

Remember to thank your hostess for a lovely time.

ualized. It is as if the artist were getting to know the characters more intimately. By now, Sendak knew instinctively what sort of dress Mother Bear would be likely to wear, and genuine affection made him see the bear family in the most flattering light. The final illustration for *Little Bear's Visit* is one of the most appealing pictures in the five-book series. Little Bear has just spent an exciting and tiring day visiting Grandmother and Grandfather Bear. Mother Bear and Father Bear arrive at last to take him home, but he has fallen asleep and must be carried by Father Bear. The three generations of the bear family appear before us at once: we can see the resemblance between Mother Bear and her own mother; we clearly read age in the elder bears' faces, figures, and postures. It is a thoroughly believable and poignant moment—revealing a gifted artist's true magic. The illustrations for Jack Sendak's *Circus Girl* (one of a half-dozen tales published by the artist's brother in the late fifties and early sixties) make dramatic use of a blue tone over black drawing to provide just the right dreamlike, mildly melancholy mood for the tale; the best of them have an almost Tenniel-like charm.

In black-and-white, Sendak's increasing mastery is evident in the drawings done for Meindert DeJong's *The House of Sixty Fathers*. They possess a conviction and weight not present earlier in his career. The picture of the book's hero seated in a round tub, his mother bending over him, helping him wash, is worthy of Seurat.

Virtuosity in a lighter vein can be found in Sendak's two-book collaboration with Sesyle Joslin, *What Do You Say, Dear?* and *What Do You Do, Dear?* Parodies of Victorian primers on infant deportment, the books owe their playful charm to

Above: from What Do You Do, Dear?. *1961. Pen-and-ink line, with two wash separations. 6⅞ x 16½".* *Opposite: from* The Moon Jumpers. *1959. Tempera. 10 x 14¼"*

Sendak's deadpan little hero and heroine, who manage to speak and act in precisely the proper manner, whether confronted by a dragon at a birthday party or a crocodile out for an afternoon stroll. Though Sendak maintained the same general style in both books, the passage of three years between books resulted in a surer, bolder hand in the latter work.

Sendak did *What Do You Say, Dear?* for a publishing house other than Harper. Because he knew both the publisher, William Scott, of Young Scott Books, and the book's editor, he was eager to take the assignment. He also felt that the time had come to branch out, to gain the experience of working with other editors and publishers on a greater variety of books. Though Sendak collaborated with many authors working for different publishing houses after this first book with Young Scott, he has always done his own picture books for Harper, with Ursula Nordstrom as his editor.

Of the books he illustrated in the late 1950s, *Seven Tales*, by Hans Christian Andersen, is one that Sendak came to dislike heartily. He feels that the medieval setting he chose was both arbitrary and shallow, and that he had not yet sufficiently digested his various trips abroad to use a European background convincingly. What came out instead was, in Sendak's appraisal, "graphic whimsy." Still, there are some lovely, painterly full pages in color, as well as several spirited black-and-white line drawings and chapter decorations. In fact, his small, full-color title-page drawing of the Steadfast Tin Soldier must have pleased Sendak well enough, because he used it later, with little except background modifications, when he did the cover art for Erik C. Haugaard's translation of *The Complete Fairy Tales & Stories of Andersen*.

His illustrations for Janice May Udry's *The Moon Jumpers*, published in 1959, are not among his favorites either. The book is an uneasy mix of black-and-white line drawings alternating with rich, full-color paintings in deep blues, greens, and purples. Sendak today finds his performance "hollow and empty." Yet, in some subliminal way, *The Moon Jumpers* deeply influenced the mood, the palette, and even the content of the three major illustrations in *Where the Wild Things Are*.

Another of what Sendak considers "my aberration books" is Clemens Brentano's *The Tale of Gockel, Hinkel and Gackeliah*, published in 1961. When the translator, Doris Orgel, gave him the German story to read, Sendak liked it immediately, but the illustrations proved difficult for him. He was feeling the need for a change of style and wanted this book to look different. "Everything was ultrasophisticated in illustration at the time," he recalls, "and I was determined to have a new, thoroughly contemporary look. The result was too violent an effort to change the surface, without a corresponding inner response to the

Opposite: from Circus Girl. *1957. Pen-and-ink line, with three wash separations. 9⅝ x 14⅜"*

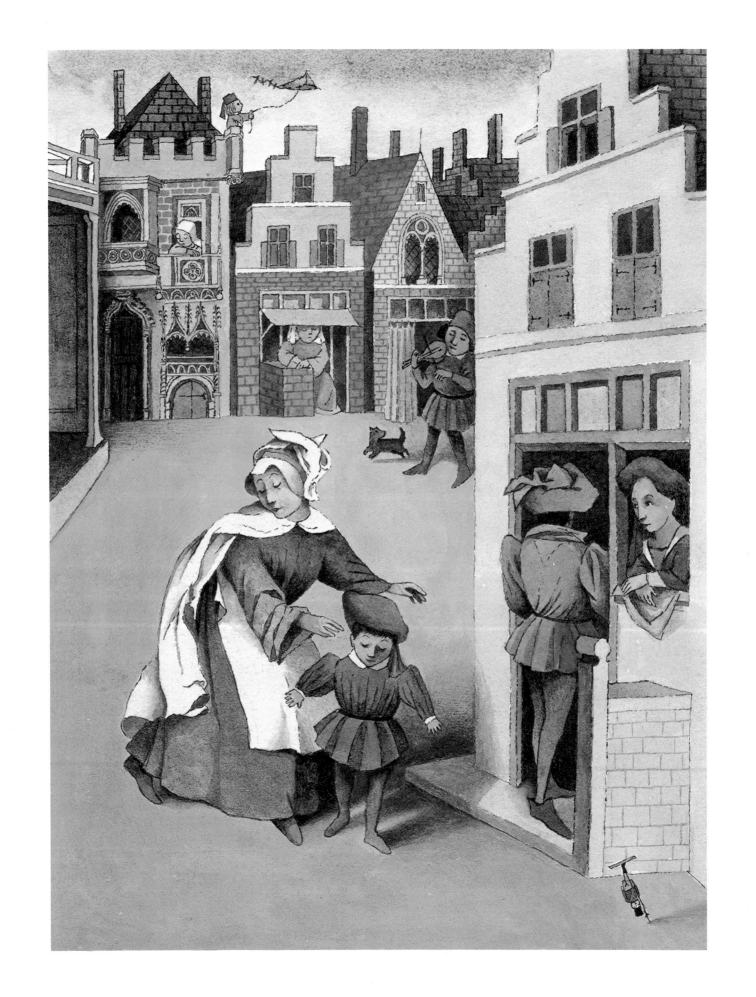

Opposite: from Seven Tales. *1959. Tempera. 8³/₄" x 6¹/₂". Above: end-papers, from* Dwarf Long-Nose. *1960. Pen-and-ink line. 8⁷/₈ x 14¹/₄"*

work and its requirements." It was a mistake Sendak was not to make again.

The artist had fared better a year earlier with another Orgel translation from the German, Wilhelm Hauff's *Dwarf Long-Nose.* From the jauntily silhouetted endpapers over which all the characters march, to the comic yet poignant characterization of the hero, the book exudes an effortless charm. Though the style of illustration closely resembles that in Andersen's *Seven Tales,* all pretension and stiffness are gone from the Old World medieval setting. The characters move through it as naturally as Sendak's sketchbook children romp on Brooklyn streets. In a second Brentano work translated by Orgel, *Schoolmaster Whackwell's Wonderful Sons,* the artist provided some of the most memorable illustrations of his career. His Giant Snorrasper, the villain of the tale, has just enough of the ludicrous about him to keep him from terrifying small viewers.

For Charlotte Zolotow's *Mr. Rabbit and the Lovely Present,* one of the most

popular and evocative works of the early years, Sendak chose a setting in Vergennes, Vermont, where he had just spent a summer vacation. The story—about a little girl who is looking for a present for her mother and accepts help from a debonair rabbit she meets—is illustrated in soft, luminous watercolors. Though the pictures are light and airy, there is an inexplicable undertone of melancholy. The book's tender woodland scenes are reminiscent of Corot. But the dominant influence, according to the artist, was Winslow Homer, a happy accident resulting from Sendak's having visited the Sterling and Francine Clark museum in Williamstown, Massachusetts, where he saw some "remarkable small Homer watercolors." The scene in which Mr. Rabbit and the little girl sit by a river bank is borrowed compositionally and coloristically from Homer.

It is hardly surprising that Sendak's work improved markedly during this period. He illustrated more than fifty books between 1951 and 1962.

At the same time he was refining his technique in published work, the artist was moving in quite another direction in sketchbooks filled with fantasy sequences done for his own diversion. A sort of graphic calisthenics done to limber the imagination, these fantasy sketches were composed as Sendak listened to various pieces of classical music. Some highly polished, others perfunctory in execution, they comprise a kind of visual free-association process, through which the artist liberated both hand and head for the more personal works to come during his most productive decade: the sixties.

His Own Work

The first book that Sendak both wrote and illustrated was *Kenny's Window*, done when he was twenty-seven. Until then, he was unwilling to try a book of his own for lack of a worthwhile subject—a scruple that, alas, seems to trouble all too few authors of children's books today. It was the reading of *One Little Boy*, a clinical study of a disturbed and apathetic child by the psychologist Dorothy Baruch, that gave the artist the prototype and namesake for his first hero, Kenny, and a subject that would engage his talents and sensibility from that moment on: children who, in Sendak's words, "are held back by life, but, one way or another, manage miraculously to find release from their troubles." The subject matter was particularly congenial to him at the time, for he was undergoing psychoanalysis and becoming increasingly aware of the wellsprings in childhood of our deepest desires and

Opposite: from Mr. Rabbit and the Lovely Present. *1962. Watercolor. 6¹¹/₁₆ x 7¹⁵/₁₆"*

7. do you always want what you think you want?

From Kenny's Window.
*1956. Pen-and-ink line,
with two wash separations.
8⅜ x 10¹/₁₆″*

fears. The new author dedicated his maiden effort to his parents, his editor Ursula Nordstrom, and his analyst.

The writing of this first book did not come easily. Sendak was spending the summer of 1955 in West Cornwall, Connecticut—where he had been each summer since 1952—at Yelping Hill, a community of writers on the property of the editor Henry Seidel Canby and his wife. Sendak remembers Ursula Nordstrom's coming there and remaining a few days to help him with the *Kenny* manuscript. "We would walk in the woods and talk about what I was trying to say. She was endlessly patient and immensely helpful."

Looked at today, *Kenny's Window* is a dreamlike and tentative evocation of the new kind of hero and heroine Sendak would introduce to young children's books. Though the story is overlong and overwritten, it is a treasure trove of the themes, situations, and psychological excursions that would become the core of Sendak's mature work. Kenny wakes from a dream in which a four-legged rooster has posed seven cryptic questions: *Can you draw a picture on the blackboard when somebody doesn't want you to? What is an only goat? Can you hear a horse on the roof? Can you fix a broken promise? What is a very narrow escape? What looks inside and what looks outside? Do you always want what you think you want?* If only the small hero can find the right answers, he will be able to live in a magical garden where the sun and moon shine simultaneously, and where he will never have to go to bed—i.e., a place in which he will not be subject to the confines of a child's world; a place where, possibly, he will never have to die (being made to go to bed is often viewed by small children as a form of annihilation).

Though Kenny is not especially brave, he pluckily embarks on seven separate adventures in quest of answers. In one, he must placate his teddy bear, Bucky, whose feelings have been hurt; in another, he travels in Switzerland via "a little train that climbed straight up the side of a mountain" to locate an only goat; in yet another, he finds himself in philosophical discourse with his dog—a Sealyham, like the author's own pet, Jennie—who is here called "Baby." *Kenny's Window* distills much of the emotional climate of Sendak's own childhood, with his deep attachment to particular toys and his fantasizing about them during long hours of solitary play while convalescing from various illnesses. By the end of Kenny's story, the hero manages to come up with all seven right responses, but the search itself has proved so satisfying that he no longer wants to live in the magic garden.

If there is an overall theme in *Kenny's Window,* it is a highly ambitious one for a young author's first book: it deals with nothing less than the child's struggle to integrate his fantasies and fears with real-life experience; to have faith in his dreams and thereby gain mastery over the circumstances of his life. What's new is that Sendak permits his hero to be angry, unjust, and even cruel at times—just like children in the real world. Like all of Sendak's own books, *Kenny's Window* moves effortlessly between the real world and one of fantasy. Yet the fantasy is controlled by a tight internal logic that never leaves the young listener troubled by loose ends.

Regarding the role that imagination and make-believe play in children's lives, Sendak has said:

Fantasy is so all-pervasive—I don't think there's any part of our lives, as adults or children, when we're not fantasizing, but we prefer to relegate that activity to children, as if fantasy were some tomfoolery only fit for immature minds. Children do live in both fantasy and reality; they move back and forth with ease, in a way that we no longer remember how to do. And in writing for children I always assume that they have this incredible flexibility, this cool sense of the logic of illogic, and that they can move with me from one sphere to the other without any problems. Fantasy is the core of all writing for children, as I think it is for the writing of any book—

perhaps even for the act of living. Certainly it is crucial to my work. There are many kinds of fantasy and levels of fantasy and subtleties of fantasy—there is probably no such thing as creativity without fantasy.

On another occasion, the artist elaborated on the subject:

The qualities that make for excellence in children's literature can be sweepingly summed up in a single word: imagination. And imagination as it relates to the child is, to my mind, synonymous with fantasy. Contrary to most of the propaganda in books for the young, childhood is only partly a time of innocence. It is, in my opinion, a time of seriousness, bewilderment, and a good deal of suffering. It's also possibly the best of all times. Imagination for the child is the miraculous, freewheeling device he uses to course his way through the problems of every day. It's the normal and healthy outlet for corrosive emotions such as impotent frustration and rage; the positive and appropriate channeling of overwhelming and, to the child, inappropriate feelings. It is through fantasy that children achieve catharsis.

Sendak's spare drawings in two colors for *Kenny's Window* are considerably less memorable than the text. He is harsh in his judgment of the artwork today: "The pictures are ghastly—I really wasn't up to illustrating my own texts then. And the story itself, to be honest, is nice but long-winded."

By the time Sendak wrote and illustrated his second book, *Very Far Away,* he had greater confidence in himself as an author and elected to tell a more modest—and also more affecting—tale. The story deals with small Martin, who must come to terms with a sad and frustrating domestic truth: his mother is too busy caring for a new baby to pay attention to him when he most craves it. Martin opts to run off "very far away where somebody will answer my questions." As the Sendakian crow flies, "very far away" is "many times around the block and two cellar windows from the corner," a place where Martin and three new-found friends—a bird, a horse, and a cat—cheerfully repair. Once there, "they live together very happily for an hour and a half," reports an author with a clear idea of how small children reckon eons. At the adventure's close, a less sulky Martin, weary of his companions' bickering, runs all the way home in the hope that his mother will now have time to answer a few vital questions—like "what refined means, and why horses dream and why cats ever sing when they don't know how." Though he has been angry with his mother, Martin never confronts his feelings; he retreats instead until his rage has dissipated—which detracts from the drama and power of the tale.

Opposite: Alinda the Lovely Lady Singer, from The Sign on Rosie's Door. *1958. Pen-and-ink line, with three wash separations. 8³⁄₈ x 8¹⁄₄". Note: this reproduction, containing the chair and the page of text, was reconstructed by the artist to suggest the feeling of the original book; it is not exactly as it appears in the published work.*

They were all gone. Two of the folding chairs lay on their sides.

"It's getting late," said Kathy. "I have to go home."

"Wasn't it a wonderful show?" asked Rosie.

"It was the best I ever saw," Kathy answered. "Let's have another one soon."

"Same time, same place," said Rosie.

"Good-by, Cha-Charoo."

"Good-by, Alinda."

Rosie was all alone. She climbed on top of a folding chair and said very quietly, "Ladies and gentlemen, Alinda will now sing 'On the Sunny Side of the Street.' "

And she sang the song all the way to the end.

The two-color artwork for this second book is direct and lighthearted, more relaxed than that of *Kenny's Window*. It displays the humor characteristic of the artist's illustrations for the work of other authors. Sendak even incorporated a picture of himself walking his dog Jennie. Though he considers Martin "fussy and sulking and not very brave," Sendak shows great sympathy for his hero's plight—Martin's feeling of abandonment now that a second child occupies so much of his mother's time.

Sendak's third book, *The Sign on Rosie's Door*, developed out of an unfocused first manuscript, "Rosie's Show," which Sendak had begun writing in 1949. The published work finds a still more self-assured artist lovingly casting the real Rosie in a slice-of-Brooklyn-life drama. With the brass and bravura of a budding Barbra Streisand, the irrepressible Rosie carries her less imaginative cronies aloft on therapeutic flights of fancy. Thanks to her, they are able to defeat the boredom of a long summer day by attending a command performance by "Alinda, the lovely lady singer" (the book was originally to have carried this "stage name" as its title); they impatiently await the mystery-shrouded arrival of Magic Man; and, at last, they themselves become phizzing, whizzing firecrackers in a bang-up Fourth of July finale. Sendak still looks fondly on this work as a major advance in his lifelong exploration of the ways in which children turn to fantasy as a means of escaping their daily troubles—in this case, endless stretches of vacation time with "nothing to do."

Beyond this, the book has a more serious underlying theme. When Sendak first sketched the original Rosie from his window during 1948 and 1949, he mar-

Above: sketches of Sendak's niece Barbara as Alinda the Lovely Lady Singer and as Rosie. 1960. Pen-and-ink line. Each sketch 11 x 8½". Opposite: Rosie sketches, from a Brooklyn sketchbook. 1947. Pen-and-ink line. Each figure 8⅛ x 5¼"

veled at the way in which she "forced her fantasies" on her more pedestrian friends; he even credited "the tremendous energy she put into these dream games" with activating his own creativity. Rosie was a fierce child who could imagine herself into being anything she wanted to be—anywhere in or out of the world. She was, in sum, an artist; and beneath the surface plot and incidents concerning a group of children and their victory over boredom, Sendak's tale is a meditation on the role of art, and on the artist's life. The Rosie of his story entertains her friends and enriches their lives, but only up to a point. In the end, they leave her to do other things and she is left alone with her creativity. Rosie is desperately vulnerable. She depends on an audience for appreciation and stimulation, yet, like all artists, she can hold its attention only so long. Ultimately, she creates because she must; she is an admirable but isolated figure.

The three-color illustrations in *The Sign on Rosie's Door* are richer in emotional content and sense of locale than those in either *Very Far Away* or *Kenny's Window*. Drawn, in part, from memory and those "out-my-window" sketchbooks of a dozen years before, the drawings of Rosie as performer, particularly, are full of loving humor and affection. Their liveliness is enhanced by the fact that the artist did a series of action sketches specifically for the book, posing his niece Barbara and his nephew Seth (Natalie's children) as Alinda and Lenny.

Sendak's next work, published in 1962, was a highly polished quartet, the perennially popular miniature volumes of his *Nutshell Library*. This included a reptilian alphabet, *Alligators All Around*; a seasons book, *Chicken Soup with Rice*; a forward-and-backward counting rhyme, *One Was Johnny*; and a delectable contemporary cautionary tale, *Pierre*. Each of these verse works is almost irresistibly memorizable. The fanciful foursome has been referred to by one critic as a young listener's "Compleat Companion to Literacy." Another proclaimed the illustrator to be "the Picasso of children's books." These small works, about 2½ by 4 inches in size, allowed Sendak to show just how much a gifted artist could fit felicitously into a confining format, breathing fresh life into subject matter already done to a fare-thee-well in the literature of childhood.

The peculiar genesis of these tiny books is worth noting. Sometime late in 1960, a nursery-school teacher sent to Miss Nordstrom at Harper a batch of stories that had been dictated to her by her small charges. "The work was mostly what you'd expect from four-year-olds," Miss Nordstrom says, "but there was one piece that captivated me. It was called 'A Cheerful Story by Alice,' and its text read something like: 'A bird didn't die, / A cat didn't catch it, / A car didn't hit it, / A train didn't run over it. / And that's the end of my cheerful story.'" Miss Nordstrom tried to discover the full identity of the author and planned to ask her

A *a* ALLIGATORS
ALL AROUND----

B *b* BEHIND BOOKCASES

C *c* CHASING CATS

D *d* DOING DISHES

E *e* EATING EVERYTHING

F *f* FOREVER FOOLING

G *g* GETTING GRUMPY

H *h* HAVING HEADACHES

I *i* IMITATING INDIANS

J *j* JUMPING JUMPROPE

K *k* KEEPING KANGAROOS

L *l* LOOKING LIKE LIONS

PIERRE

A CAUTIONARY TALE

IN FIVE CHAPTERS

AND A PROLOGUE

by MAURICE SENDAK

HARPER + BROTHERS, EST. 1817

SEPT. 11, 61

Opposite: working dummy for Alligators All Around. *1961. Pen-and-ink line and watercolor. 10½ x 9″. Above: title pages from dummy for* Pierre. *1961. Pen-and-ink line and watercolor. 3½ x 5″*

parents' permission to use the text for "a very little book." But by the time she had written to the teacher, Alice was no longer in the class and couldn't be located. The project was thus abandoned, "but the idea of a little book remained in our heads in the children's department," Miss Nordstrom recalls. "One day I told the story to Maurice, and he was taken with the notion of trying a miniature-size volume, with story to match. The result, of course, was more wonderful than anything we could have imagined, and it was Ferdinand Monjo, another Harper editor at the time, who thought of the inspired overall title *The Nutshell Library*."

Quintessentially Sendak, *Alligators All Around* finds an amiable family of three alligators journeying joyously from A to Z. Whether "D doing dishes," "R riding reindeer," or "X x-ing x's," they are single-mindedly devoted to the activity at hand, encouraging the young listener/viewer to learn each alliterative alphabetical label. Effortless as the little book seems, it went through a number of drafts. The alligators started their literary life as a family of apes in Sendak's first version. Says the author, "The least important aspect of *Alligators* is that it is an alphabet. I wanted to see how much I could get away with in a form that is so fixed and

71

8 was a tiger out selling old clothes

stilted. My alligators aren't teachers: they're like my later hero Max in *Where the Wild Things Are*. They stick their tongues out, stand upside down, and are very vain. They do the kind of things that all my children do." In *One Was Johnny*, Sendak wreaks cumulative havoc; to the count of one to ten and back again, on the hermetic lifestyle of a little boy who "lived by himself and liked it that way." Another small boy romps through the pages of *Chicken Soup with Rice*, in and out of all the months of the year, fueled by frequent infusions of the title's restorative liquid elixir. Probably the best known of the quartet, *Chicken Soup* is dedicated to Ida Perles, a neighbor and close friend during the early Brooklyn days whom the three Sendak children always looked upon as a second mother. It was Mrs. Perles's unshakeable belief in the curative powers of loving care and good home cooking that inspired the work. Then, tongue-in-cheek, the author gives us *Pierre*, the tale of a languid, misanthropic lad jolted into harmony with the rest of humanity after a salubrious sojourn inside the stomach of a hungry lion. The only one of the four books that contains no dedication to an old friend, *Pierre* is closest to Sendak's heart; the book may well be implicitly dedicated to the author himself.

Above: from One Was Johnny. *1962. Pen-and-ink line, with three wash separations. 3 x 4½".*
Opposite: painting for the slipcase of The Nutshell Library. *1962. Pen-and-ink line and watercolor. 10⁷⁄₁₆ x 8⅛"*

Left: from Pierre. *1962. Pen-and-ink line, with three wash separations. 3 x 2¼". Right: from* Chicken Soup with Rice. *1962. Pen-and-ink line, with three wash separations. 3¼ x 2⁷/₁₆"*

In terms of bookmaking—the happy amalgam of text, drawings, and design—the four little books represent a marked advance over Sendak's three earlier books. The complete set is boxed in a simulated wooden crate decorated by the artist, with mock-curtained openings on the sides and back, revealing small stages which display characters from each book. In terms of overall conception and execution, *Pierre* is the most ambitious and the handsomest of the little books. Its contents page and five chapters begin with tiny rectangular tableaus, giving the reader a playful preview of what lies ahead. Since publication, the boxed set of *The Nutshell Library* has sold nearly a half-million copies. Each of the individual titles has been published in a larger-format library edition. These have had a combined sale of almost a quarter-million copies, with *Chicken Soup with Rice* leading the rest in popularity.

Though the books all seem spontaneous and lightly tossed off, their early dummies reveal that there were significant changes in the pictures, as well as alterations in many of the verses: "B bursting balloons," for example, in *Alligators All Around* was a last-minute change. Sendak's small dummies for his books are the battlefield on which he struggles to bring words and pictures into a harmonious synchronization. He pencils in the text to appear on each page and does rough sketches of his illustrations; he also works out the graphic transitions from action to action that the words require. Usually, he has a clear idea in mind of how each page will look—what pictures go where, which way the figures in each illustration must face, what final size and shape everything should be—before he even sets pencil to paper.

If there is a common denominator to be found in these first books written by Sendak, it is that they all are about children being themselves. The stories are intended to entertain young listeners, to be sure, but the artist's heroes and heroines also engage their audience's feelings in a way new to books for small children. Kenny is at times angry, vindictive, and plagued by guilt; Martin is actively unhappy with having to play second fiddle to a demanding new baby; and Rosie is brash, bossy—a royal pain to her less driven peers at times. There is an emotional texture and complexity refreshingly respectful of, and genuinely in touch with, the often painful realities of young children's lives. Feelings are all-important. If there is a common failing in the stories, it is that they have a hazy quality—a tentativeness and lack of dramatic conflict—as if their author had not yet sharply defined, or come to grips head-on with, his subject matter. In *Kenny's Window*, we have both an indistinct protagonist and a shadowy situation. The reader has no idea what the small hero's life is like, what sort of relationship he has with his parents, whether or not he has brothers, sisters, or many friends. We know him only through his games and conversations with his toys, through his fantasy life. In *Very Far Away*, while the central situation is well defined by the author, any sense of genuine drama, conflict, or resolution is absent from the tale, possibly even intentionally avoided. Martin himself is a vague character who retreats from any confrontation with his anger, distracting himself with new friends in a new place. With *The Sign on Rosie's Door*, Sendak presents his first fully realized character; but Rosie, like Martin, is the star of an episodic and diffuse story. Her compelling make-believe is diverting and useful, so far as it goes, but she is heroine on an ever so small stage. Her tale is long on charm but short on power. Even *The Nutshell Library*'s Pierre, who is closest in spirit and spunk to Sendak's best-known heroes of the sixties, exists in a kind of limbo. "Why doesn't he care?" the reader might well ask, were the humor not so deliciously diverting, the situation of being swallowed by a lion so mesmerizingly scary.

With the publication of *The Nutshell Library*, Sendak had illustrated fifty books, seven of which he had also written. He was thirty-four years old and restless for new challenges, and his apprenticeship was coming to an end.

A Controversial Triumph

Where the Wild Things Are

A great illustrator, like a major painter, musician, or dancer, can never be accounted for in terms of talent alone. There are always crucial variables—among them application, ambition, capacity for continuing spiritual and technical growth, experience, luck, and sustained interest by the artist in the particular art form. So far as experience is concerned, Sendak had provided pictures for an impressive number and variety of young children's books by the end of 1962. Some of these works are slight and would, in all likelihood, have passed unnoticed were it not for his energetic and highly personalized contribution. Others, like Krauss's *A Hole Is to Dig* or Minarik's *Little Bear* books, have an innate strength and charm that called upon his untapped reserves of concentration, originality, and purposeful attention to the achievements of great illustrators of the past. If the artist's confidence required any further bolstering by 1962, the great popular success of his *Nutshell Library*, following the respectful reception of the three earlier books he had written as well as illustrated, convinced him that he could now devote his efforts to projects of his own choosing: either challenging tales from the classical repertoire of children's literature or, in time, a full-color picture book of his own. He longed to exercise his preferences and taste. But this goal could not be realized immediately. Sendak had several illustrating commitments to fulfill during 1963, among them *She Loves Me, She Loves Me Not*, by Robert Keeshan (better known to countless millions of young children as Captain Kangaroo); *How Little Lori Visited Times*

Opposite: detail (see page 84) from Where the Wild Things Are. *1963. Pen-and-ink line and water-color. Above: sketch for* Where the Wild Things Are. *Pencil. 3½ x 3¾"*

Opposite: from The Griffin and the Minor Canon. *1963. Pen-and-ink line, with three wash separations. 7¹¹⁄₁₆ x 7³⁄₁₆″. Above: from* She Loves Me, She Loves Me Not. *Pen-and-ink line, with three wash separations. Each 3⁹⁄₁₆ x 3³⁄₈″*

Square, by Amos Vogel; *Sarah's Room*, by Doris Orgel; *Nikolenka's Childhood*, by Leo Tolstoy; and *The Griffin and the Minor Canon*, by Frank Stockton.

She Loves Me, She Loves Me Not is a soufflé of a picture book in the vein of several of Sendak's fifties collaborations—Ruth Krauss's *A Very Special House* and Beatrice de Regnier's *What Can You Do with a Shoe?*, among others. The artist's by-now-familiar boy and girl principals enact a pantomime/melodrama, alternating between elation and despair as each, in turn, plucks the petals of a daisy—"She loves me…She loves me not." Above the children's heads, a pair of scene-stealing cupids echo the shifting moods of hero and heroine, until, at last, the aye-petals win out. It is not a book Sendak thinks much of today; "its raison d'être was simply to make money," he says dismissively.

In *How Little Lori Visited Times Square*, the artist turns author Vogel's intended comedy-of-errors into a kind of nightmare of childhood frustration. Lori, the small hero, attempts to reach Times Square on his own, but he is thwarted at every turn. He gets on the wrong bus, train, and even boat. (Sendak christens the ferry that Lori mistakenly takes to Staten Island the *Grampus*, after the ill-fated ship in Edgar Allan Poe's tale of horror *The Narrative of Arthur Gordon Pym*.) Even when Lori at last entrusts himself to a turtle who definitely knows the way to Times Square and the two set out confidently, there is no assurance given to the reader

that they ever reach their destination. Though the author informs his young audience at the outset that this is a funny story (and, therefore, one not to be read while drinking orange juice), the illustrator so feelingly depicts the small hero's frustrating predicament that the listener cannot help but be a bit queasy at the tongue-in-cheek ending. Adults have no trouble catching the author's joke about the turtle's notoriously slow pace, but perhaps some children are left worrying about what has happened to Lori. It is not the sort of story that Sendak—who has strong feelings about tying up all loose ends in children's books—would himself have written.

A thoroughly harmonious collaboration, by contrast, was *Sarah's Room*, a small-format, deliberately old-fashioned-looking book in which the little heroine, Jenny, finds herself banished from her older sister's room because she is too young and irresponsible to take proper care of the dolls and toys in residence there. A lock is placed on Sarah's door, above the younger sibling's reach. Jenny takes her revenge by invading the premises in a dream—she can now fly into the forbidden chamber. Sendak's pictures of the naughty Jen drawing on her own wall and, later, levitated to latch-level of sister Sarah's door, are full of sympathetic humor. Once again, Sendak uses a Victorian setting to enhance the flavor and point of the tale. Somehow, a contemporary child's bedroom could never have the same aura of

Above: from How Little Lori Visited Times Square. *1963. Pen-and-ink line, with three wash separations. 5¼ x 14⅞".* *Opposite: facsimile of seven of the original sixteen pages, and photograph of the earliest dummy for* Where the Wild Things Are. *1955. Pen-and-ink line and watercolor. ¾ x 7"*

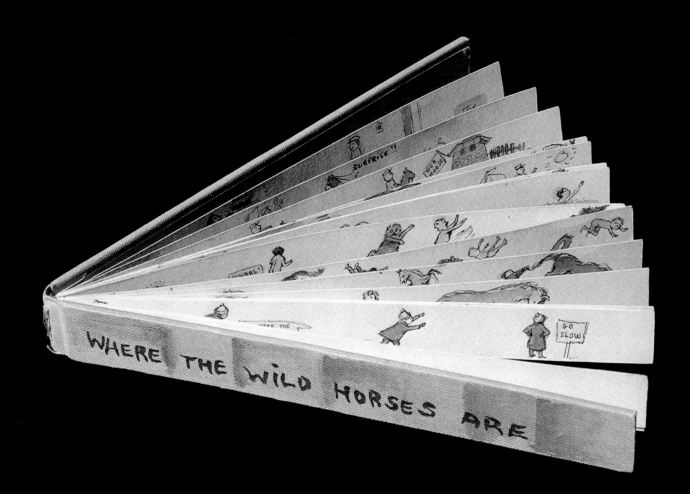

tempting untouchability as Sarah's perfectly ordered, period-piece bedchamber. Slightly larger in size than the volumes of *The Nutshell Library*, this sweet—but never cloying—work is in the same cautionary-tale tradition as *Pierre*. Here, the message is that responsible behavior merits special privileges.

Tolstoy's *Nikolenka's Childhood* opened Sendak's eyes to the limits of illustration. He had been eager for the assignment, but found, once he had begun the pictures, that there was little he could bring to the text that the author himself had not already achieved with words. "It was one of Tolstoy's first novellas, and it is great," he says. "But Tolstoy, like all great writers, is his own illustrator. When he describes a mother's death and her child's bereavement, heaven knows you don't need a picture. Tolstoy spells it out for the reader in ways that are terribly painful; he leaves no room for pictures. I did a fairly decent job, I suppose, but halfway through the story I realized that I truly wanted to have written it, not to illustrate it at all. Essentially, what I did added nothing to Tolstoy's remarkably visual writing." Sendak's father, however, was impressed and proud that his son had been chosen to do pictures for a work by so illustrious an author. "Does this mean," he asked the artist, "that they'll let you illustrate real books now?"

With *The Griffin and the Minor Canon*, Sendak found himself a most congenial turn-of-the-century American writer, Frank Stockton. Though he had read Stockton's adult short story *The Lady or the Tiger?* in high school, the artist knew none of the delightful, imaginative tales for children that Stockton had written—mostly for the *St. Nicholas* magazine—in the 1870s and 1880s. Probably this country's best writer of fairy stories, Stockton had wit, style, and a lightness of touch often conspicuously lacking in his younger and far better known colleague L. Frank Baum. For a while, Stockton worked with editor Mary Mapes Dodge (author of *Hans Brinker, or the Silver Skates*) putting out the first issues of *St. Nicholas*, and it is to their joint efforts that this unparalleled children's magazine owed its unique and patrician character. "Reading *The Griffin and the Minor Canon* was very much like opening a treasure chest," Sendak wrote in his introduction to the work. "What a gold mine of pictorial possibilities! And it provided a thoroughly fascinating series of illustrating problems. I wanted at all costs to avoid the serious pitfall of illustrating with pictures what the author had already—and so wonderfully—illustrated with words [shades of Sendak's unhappy experience with *Nikolenka's Childhood*]. I hoped, rather, to let the story speak for itself, with my pictures as a kind of background music, music in the right style, in the best taste, and always in tune with the words."

A lighthearted tale about the world's last surviving griffin, who comes to pay a visit to the stone image of himself in a small cathedral town in "a faraway land,"

From Sarah's Room.
*1963. Pen-and-ink line,
with three wash separations.
4³/₈ x 5¹⁵/₁₆"*

it needed an equally light touch in the artwork. Comparing the convincingly European background in *The Griffin and the Minor Canon* with its theatrical-set counterpart in *Seven Tales*, by Hans Christian Andersen, reveals how far Sendak had advanced in four years. In the Stockton work, both the Old World cathedral town and its citizens are entirely believable, as is the griffin who takes up unwelcome residence in their midst. Sendak's black-and-white illustrations, crosshatched within sharp outlines, dominate the three-color artwork, giving to the book a genuinely nineteenth-century look. It is a happy collaboration, and certainly the artist's full-page drawing of the irascible griffin taking the temperature of a terrified child is memorably scary and funny. The scale of griffin to child is perfect for max-

83

imum dramatic impact. The illustration of the dutiful young canon leading the griffin to his stone image at the cathedral's entrance is likewise a felicitous amalgam of comedy and menace. The griffin's threatening size, the canon's resigned posture—was there ever a more unlikely pair?

By the time Sendak decided to try a picture book of his own, he was already on comfortable terms with the broad theme that would dominate his own writing: "My great curiosity about childhood as a state of being, and how all children manage to get through childhood from one day to the next, how they defeat boredom, fear, pain, and anxiety, and find joy. It is a constant miracle to me that children manage to grow up." He considered none of his own work up to this point— *Kenny's Window*, *Very Far Away*, *The Sign on Rosie's Door*, or the foursome of *The Nutshell Library*—to be picture books. The length and content of their texts placed them in the category of illustrated books, works in which words carry decidedly more weight than pictures and illustration serves merely to heighten the narrative's forward motion. By contrast, the picture book is a form unto itself, a special mix of text and art, in which the pictures are vitally needed to fill in what the words leave unsaid; the words, in turn, are indispensable to moving the narrative forward during whatever time—or space—gaps exist between illustrations. In a picture book, neither text nor pictures by themselves can tell the story. They comprise an equal and totally interdependent partnership.

Sendak had several fragmentary situations in mind for his first picture book, but when he began to write, the texts seemed to grow longer and longer. He used some of his favorite picture books as models, among them the English artist William Nicholson's *The Pirate Twins*, written in 1929. As to where the specific idea for *Where the Wild Things Are* came from, Sendak explains, "None of my books come about through 'ideas,' or by thinking of a particular subject and exclaiming, 'Gee, that's terrific; I'll just put it down!' They never happen quite that way. They well up. Just as dreams come to us at night, feelings come to me, and I rush to put them down. But these fantasies have to be given a physical form, so I build a kind of house around them—the story—and the painting of the house is the picture-making. Essentially, however, it's a dream or fantasy." But all successful fantasy, Sendak points out repeatedly, "must be rooted in living fact." In *Where the Wild Things Are*, the hero's adventure among the wild things is preceded by the real-life fact of his rage against his mother—which is precipitated by another fact: he has been sent to bed without any supper.

The book opens on Max, a child of four or five, dressed in his wolf suit (a quasi-pajama/Halloween outfit) making "mischief of one kind and another." He chases the dog down the stairs and, when his mother calls him "Wild Thing!" he

Opposite: from Where the Wild Things Are. *1963. Pen-and-ink line and watercolor. 4⁷⁄₈ x 6³⁄₁₆"*

responds, "I'll eat you up!" Banished to his bedroom with nothing to eat, an angry Max, eyes closed, virtually wills his room to change into a forest. (Even the bedposts are magically transformed into trees.) When the small hero intrepidly enters this fantasy forest, he discovers a boat that delivers him to the place where the wild things are. Undaunted on meeting the monsters—who are, once again, a Sendakian blend of menace and make-believe—Max has no trouble charming the terrible beasts by staring unblinkingly into their terrible eyes. After a wild rumpus of dancing and shouting, which he leads, Max grows homesick when "from far away across the world he smelled good things to eat." He leaves the wild things behind, and, retracing his route, arrives home to a happy surprise: his supper is waiting for him—"and it was still hot."

The original fantasy for *Where the Wild Things Are* had been set down in November 1955, when Sendak completed a long, thin, horizontal dummy which he titled "Where the Wild Horses Are." In this earliest version, a small boy follows an arrow "To Where the Wild Horses Are." As he moves closer to his destination, he comes upon three other markers that warn: "Go Slow," "Don't Let Them See You," and "Hide Your Eyes," almost like the run-on Burma Shave advertising signs seen along the highways in the thirties and forties. Once the boy arrives at where the wild horses are, he is kicked out of his clothes by the untamed animals; then, as he continues walking, nude and pathetically vulnerable-looking, he is pursued consecutively by a running monster, a flying bird, and a wolf. To escape from these creatures, he jumps into a convenient body of water, where he finds a boat. He sets sail for Happy Island, where he disembarks and finds a small bride waiting for him in a little house. Max, the hero of *Wild Things*, finds instead his supper waiting for him at the end of his trip, the perfect reward for a no-longer-angry little boy eager for reconciliation with his mother.

Wild Things uses less than half the material in the 1955 *Wild Horses* dummy, but Sendak's pictures so expand the simple, 338-word text that the artist has made of it probably the most suspenseful and satisfying nursery tale of our time. Essentially, the strength of *Wild Things* lies in the author's injection of strong emotion and motivation. In *Wild Horses*, the hero simply ambles into a forest following an arrow. But Max leaves his bedroom because of his rage at his mother. And the young reader's feelings are deeply engaged from the start. Much of Sendak's lean narrative has the lilt of free verse: "And he sailed off through night and day / and in and out of weeks / and almost over a year / to where the wild things are." The illustrations are wondrously authoritative and alive, which, the artist points out, "is not to say I've made the words less important; I simply opened up the lines in ways that at first may not have seemed possible."

Opposite: from Where the Wild Things Are. *1963. Pen-and-ink line and watercolor. 6¹³/₁₆ x 8⅛"*

87

As to how wild horses became wild things, Sendak confides:

I couldn't really draw horses. And I didn't, for the longest time, know what to use as a substitute. I tried lots of different animals in the title, but they just didn't sound right. Finally, I lit on *things*. But what would "things" look like? I wanted my wild things to be frightening. But why? It was probably at this point that I remembered how I detested my Brooklyn relatives as a small child. They came almost every Sunday, and there was my week-long anxiety about their coming the next Sunday. My mother always cooked for them, and, as I saw it, they were eating up all our food. We had to wear good clothes for these aunts, uncles, and assorted cousins, and ugly plastic covers were put over the furniture. About the relatives themselves, I remember how inept they were at making small talk with children. There you'd be, sitting on a kitchen chair, totally helpless, while they cooed over you and pinched your cheeks. Or they'd lean way over with their bad teeth and hairy noses, and say something threatening like "You're so cute I could eat you up." And I knew if my mother didn't hurry up with the cooking, they probably would. So, on one level at least, you could say that wild things are Jewish relatives.

On another level, the artist feels certain that his conception of the wild things owes a decided debt to *King Kong*, a movie he saw as a child and never forgot. In fact, long after the book was published, an old friend who collects still pictures from films of the thirties pointed out that one of the compositions from *Wild Things* was all but identical to one of the frames from *King Kong*. On her next visit, she brought the King Kong still photograph in question and Sendak remembers, "I was amazed at how alike they were, from the positioning of the monster outside his cave to the cliff he's standing on. Of course, I had no way of copying it; it must simply have imprinted itself on my brain some thirty years earlier."

The first draft of a text for *Wild Things*, dated April 24, 1963, was still called *Wild Horses*. It read:

Once a boy asked where the wild horses are.
Nobody could tell him.
So he asked himself where the wild horses are.
And he answered, they must be this way.
Luckily the way led through his own room.
He found signs pointing in the right direction.

On April 28, the artist continued the tale:

Soon his room was the beginning of a forest. The rug on his floor was the grassy path into the forest. The boy followed the path into the very middle of the forest and then lost his way.

He entered a magic garden though the sign said do not enter, and looked round the tree though the sign said do not look. He thought this might be the place where the wild horses are.

Someone appeared and said stay with me, I am your mother. That cannot be, said the boy, you do not look like my mother, and besides my mother is home waiting for me.

Above: sketch for Where the Wild Things Are. *1963. Pencil. 4⅛ x 5⁷⁄₁₆".* *Overleaf: from* Where the Wild Things Are. *1963. Pen-and-ink line and watercolor. 6⁷⁄₁₆ x 19¾"*

89

With a growl the make-believe mother turned into a terrible wolf and chased the boy out of the magic garden, through the forest....

In a moment the boy grew to an old man and frightened the wolf away. I am now an old man, said the boy, and I have still not come to where the wild horses are. And besides, I am tired.

The idea of a mother who turns into a wolf is, of course, far more frightening than anything that finally appeared in *Wild Things*. It almost certainly accounts for Max's costume being a wolf suit, however. (Metamorphoses of one character into another—a baby into a pig, a boy into an old man, a small girl into a prima ballerina—were common occurrences in Sendak's earlier fantasy sketches, though this is the closest the artist ever came to using the concept in one of his picture books.) By May 16, 1963, Sendak had completed a typescript of the story, much as we know it today.

Once the artist had his text, he worked out a full set of pencil drawings. The sketch for the original opening page ("The night Max wore his wolf suit...") revealed a monster quilt on Max's improvised clothesline-tent. This was changed to a floral quilt in the final drawing, a far likelier child's bed-covering. (The only early hint of monsters to come is Max's drawing tacked to the wall.) The tent Max made for himself was also modified. The first sketch included an electric lamp inside the tent; this disappeared—a possible fire hazard?—in later renditions. Perhaps Sendak merely found the drawing too cluttered. All refinements in his illustrations move toward simplification. An early sketch, for example, finds Max chasing both a small dog and a younger sister at the story's start. Only the dog (Jennie, once again) remains in the final version. Also, in the earliest dummy, the artist shows Max being welcomed home to supper by the dog, but the animal is absent from this climactic moment in the final drawing. She would have been an unnecessary distraction from the all-important supper that Max's forgiving mother had left for him. Sendak's recollection is that Miss Nordstrom's suggestions dealt solely with the text; any changes or modifications in the drawings were his own.

Max's homemade tent is echoed in his fantasy when, as king of all wild things, he is given his very own, elegant tent. Sendak uses every possible link between the reality and fantasy sides of Max's tale. When, for example, the hero is banished to his room and "that very night in Max's room a forest grew...," there is absolute magic in the four posts of Max's bed turning into trees, and the pile of his rug coming alive as grass. His ceiling, too, is soon obscured by the flourishing vegetation, and, though we see a crescent moon through Max's window, the wall coloring has altered subtly to a darker, night blue, and the distinction between in- and outdoors rapidly fades. Once Max reaches the land of the wild things, the trees there are reassuringly just like those sprouting in his bedroom at home. The illustration in which the small hero (whose mother had called *him* "Wild Thing!") tames the real McCoy—five wild things—by "staring into all their yellow eyes without blinking once," shows the fierce hero at his bravest. Exactly the same crescent moon that Max sees from his own bedroom window shines on the island of the wild things. It is pictorial details like these that small children are quick to notice and appreciate; they help to give *Where the Wild Things Are* its resonance and absolute credibility.

Though Sendak today scorns the illustrations he did for Janice May Udry's *The Moon Jumpers* in 1959 as "free, painterly, and empty," certainly those richly colored pictures—in deep purples, greens, and blues—of children dancing by moonlight (see page 57) greatly influenced the mood, colors, and even the pacing of the commanding double-page "rumpus" scenes in *Where the Wild Things Are*. Just as *The Moon Jumpers* had three wordless spreads of full-color bleed (no white margins) pictures at the dramatic highpoint of the tale, so does *Wild Things*. Even the poses of the figures in both works are strikingly similar.

These three double-page orgy scenes probably comprise the best-thumbed pages in contemporary children's literature. In the first, Max and four large wild things dance and bay at the moon. Max, wearing his crown, is clearly a fit "king of all wild things." Inexplicably, a full moon now shines over their merrymaking, but at this enchanted moment no reader will quibble with the artist's lunar license. The second spread—which shifts to morning light—shows Max and his companions swinging companionably, like monkeys, from the familiar trees. In the final spread, Max is mounted triumphantly on the bristly shoulders of the wildest wild thing, and all the creatures look ecstatically happy. When Max willingly gives up his crown to sail back home "into the night of his very own room where he found his supper waiting for him," the illustration shows a smiling, spent Max, his wolf hood slipping off his head (a subtle reminder that he has been purged of his wildness and rage). On the table we see Max's supper, with a large piece of cake for dessert (suggesting that his mother has entirely forgiven him). This scene, too, is illuminated by a full moon. Of the clearly impossible lunar shifts—from crescent to full circle—Sendak says, "I love full moons. It was my old friend Tomi Ungerer who pointed out to me that my books are full of discrepancies. Full moons go to three-quarters and even halves without reason. But the moon appears in my books for graphic, not astronomical, reasons—I simply must have that shape on the page."

Several critics have commented on the way in which the *Wild Things* illustra-

Overleaf: from Where the Wild Things Are. *1963. Pen-and-ink line and watercolor. 9 x 19³/₄"*

tions grow in size as the drama unfolds. This was an intentional device to hold the reader's interest. "A picture book can be very boring," Sendak points out. "You turn one page after another, and that's it. If you are an adult you may do it without complaining. But children are not so polite. One of the reasons why the picture book is so fascinating is that there are lots of devices to make the form itself more interesting. In *Where the Wild Things Are*, the device is a matching of sizes and shapes. I used it to describe Max's moods pictorially: his anger, more or less normal in the beginning, expands into rage; then the explosion of fantasy serves as a release from that particular anger; and finally there is the gradual collapse of the fantasy and it's all over. The smell of food brings Max back to reality; he's a little boy again. A book is inert. What I try to do is animate it, make it move emotionally."

The completed dummy that Sendak submitted to Harper and Row contained three verses that varied significantly from the final printed text. They occurred just after Max smells "good things to eat" and decides to leave the wild things, despite their protests:

> But Max didn't care because the Wild Things
> never loved him best of all—or let him
> eat from grown-up plates

> or showed him how to call long distance.
> So Max gave up being King of Where the Wild Things Are.

> Wild Things are child things,"
> said Max as he steered his boat
> back over the year and in and
> out of weeks and through the day.

All three verses suffer from over-specificity, the spelling out of mundane details in a heavy-handed way. In the last, "Wild Things are child things" is a smug sentiment, completely out of character with Max. The line also has the effect of undermining the magnitude of Max's victory over the wild things; it sabotages the high seriousness of the author/artist's fantasy as well.

In his final revision of these weak lines, Sendak deleted most of the offending phrases, retaining only "loved him best of all," in a new and positive context. "And Max the king of all wild things was lonely and wanted to be where someone loved him best of all." No longer is the fantasy interrupted, and the new line allows for

Opposite: detail from **Where the Wild Things Are.** *1963. Pen-and-ink line and watercolor. 9 x 9⅞"*

Gatefold: from Where the Wild Things Are. *1963. Pen-and-ink line and watercolor. 6⁷/₁₆ x 19³/₄"*

Max's graceful exit to home, leaving the wild things' world intact.

One other line was revised in the final text. Sendak originally wrote of Max's first encounter with the wild things that the small hero "tamed them quick with the magic trick." A young editor at Harper, Susan Hirschman, was bothered by the internal rhyme. "It somehow brought the text down," she felt. So, nervously, she phoned the author and told him her reservation. After a fifteen-minute discussion, Sendak agreed with her, and the word *quick* was deleted.

As a fantasist, Sendak brings such conviction to his illustrations—he seems to live inside their reality while working on a book—that a nursery work of the imagination like *Where the Wild Things Are* seems entirely real. The artist's fantasy is not spun of gossamer; rather it seems built of bricks, made not for the moment but for the ages.

The book was published in the fall of 1963 with no special fanfare from Harper. It was only when he read the first negative letters from troubled librarians and parents that Sendak realized he had written a controversial work. Thus, the publication of *Where the Wild Things Are* turned Sendak into a sort of "Peck's bad boy" of children's books. Long recognized as a highly talented and serious artist, he had now provided children with an unquestionably beautiful but—well—scary picture book. Max gets truly angry with his mother and escapes into a dream/fantasy containing possibly terrifying wild things. Many parents, educators, and librarians were confounded, and several self-styled guardians of childhood innocence began asking questions: Would the book upset small children? Would Max's bad behavior invite young listener-viewers to emulate him? Would the wild things induce nightmares in children or be psychologically harmful in other ways?

One librarian cautioned: "It is not a book to be left where a sensitive child may come upon it at twilight." And the publishing trade magazine, *Publishers Weekly*, usually overly kind to the children's books it reviews, said of it, "The plan and technique of the illustrations are superb, but they may well prove frightening, accompanied as they are by a pointless and confusing story." The novelist Robert Phelps, writing in *Life* magazine some years after the publication of *Wild Things*, felt that the book heralded "a metamorphosis in which a skilled, professional illustrator began turning into a writer and not just another formula children's book writer, but one with a very personal obsessive vision." On nonliterary grounds, the eminent child psychologist Bruno Bettelheim wrote about *Wild Things* in the *Ladies Home Journal*: "The basic anxiety of the child is desertion. To be sent to bed alone is one desertion, and without food is the second desertion. The combination is the worst desertion that can threaten a child." At the time he made these comments, he had not read the book for himself but had simply been told its plot. A child

Opposite: from Where the Wild Things Are. *1963. Pen-and-ink line and watercolor. 9 x 9⅞"*

104

psychoanalyst in New York wrote more positively about the book: "*Where the Wild Things Are* projects, releases, and masters a universal experience for the child: the wish to eat others, the fear of eating others or of being eaten oneself. If some children are frightened by the book, it is because they are either too young or too weak (i.e. ill or disturbed). Then the fantasy of rage that is released is too much for them."

Apparently even Sendak's editor Ursula Nordstrom had certain reservations about the acceptance of *Wild Things* on first seeing the pictures. But soon afterward, she wrote Sendak: "It is always the adults we have to contend with—most children under the age of ten will react creatively to the best work of a truly creative person. But too often adults sift their reactions to creative picture books through their own adult experiences. And, as an editor who stands between the creative artist and the creative child, I am constantly terrified that I will react as a dull adult. But at least I try to remember this every minute."

Yet, despite controversy that has never been entirely resolved, *Wild Things* became an unprecedented success. It has been published in thirteen foreign language editions, including Danish, Japanese, Afrikaans, and Welsh. It also appeared in a pirated Latin edition issued by the students of Mamaroneck High School in 1972. ("Et nunc, Maximus clamorit"—runs the line as King Max orders the wild rumpus to begin—"ferae res incipiantur!")

In its hard-cover edition, *Where the Wild Things Are* has sold more than 700,000 copies as of this writing, and, in each six-month royalty period, this first and still most popular of Sendak's picture books sells an average of 15,000–16,000 copies. A paperback version sold only in the school market has sold an additional 1,800,000 copies.

Through the years following the book's publication, Sendak has made various answers to its critics. "Children are not always escaping from the mundane," he said on one occasion, "but from the horrific—from all kinds of strong, frightening feelings they have; they don't really mind a little anxiety and heart failure, so long as they know it will end all right."

On the other hand, Sendak often tells of the mother who said to him: "I've read *Where the Wild Things Are* ten times to my little girl, and she screams every time." When the author asked why she continued reading it to the child, the woman answered, "But it's a Caldecott book, she ought to like it." Sendak finds such an attitude absurd. "If a kid doesn't like a book, throw it away. Children don't give a damn about awards. Why should they? We should let children choose their own books. What they don't like they will toss aside. What disturbs them too much they will not look at. And if they look at the wrong book, it isn't going to do them that much damage. We treat children in a very peculiar way, I think. We don't treat them like the strong creatures they really are."

What pleased the artist as much as anything about *Wild Things* was discovering that the book was being successfully used with autistic children. One child, who had never exhibited any sign of connection to reality, clutched the book and spoke. Others smiled and looked interestedly at the pictures. Sendak also treasures a letter from an eight-year-old boy which reads: "How much does it cost to get to where the wild things are? If it is not expensive, my sister and I would like to spend the summer there."

Perhaps Sendak's most eloquent defense of *Where the Wild Things Are* was contained in his 1964 acceptance speech for the Caldecott Medal awarded to "the most distinguished American picture book" of the previous year. "Through fantasy," the artist said:

Max, the hero of my book, discharges his anger against his mother, and returns to the real world sleepy, hungry, and at peace with himself.

Certainly we want to protect our children from new and painful experiences that are beyond their emotional comprehension and that intensify anxiety; and to a point we can prevent premature exposure to such experiences. That is obvious. But what is just as obvious—and what is too often overlooked—is the fact that from their earliest years children live on familiar terms with disrupting emotions, that fear and anxiety are an intrinsic part of their everyday lives, that they continually cope with frustration as best they can. And it is through fantasy that children achieve catharsis. It is the best means they have for taming Wild Things.

It is my involvement with this inescapable fact of childhood—the awful vulnerability of children and their struggle to make themselves King of all Wild Things—that gives my work whatever truth and passion it may have.

The Art of the Picture Book

Curiously, it had taken Sendak more than twelve years to try for himself the form for which he is best known today—the picture book. His own definition of the genre helps to explain why. "A picture book," he says, "is not only what most people think it is—an easy thing, with a lot of pictures in it, to read to small children. For me, it is a damned difficult thing to do, like working in a complicated and challenging poetic form. It demands so much that you have to be on top of the situation all the time, finally to achieve something so simple and so put together—so seamless—that it looks as if you knocked it off in no time. One stitch showing and you've lost the game."

On another occasion, Sendak explained, "There are basically two approaches to illustration. First, there is the direct, no-nonsense approach that puts the facts of the case into simple, down-to-earth images: Miss Muffet, her tuffet, curds, whey, spider, and all. Then there is, for want of a better term, illumination. As with a poem set to song, in which every shade and nuance is given greater meaning by the music, so pictures can interpret texts." In much the same way that his favorite American author, Henry James, had spoken of his commitment to the writing of novels, Sendak says, "To me, illustrating means having a passionate affair with the words. I hate to say that it's akin to a mystic rite, but there is no other language to describe what happens. It is a sensual, deeply important experience. An illustration is an enlargement, an interpretation of the text, so that the child will comprehend the words better. As an artist, you are always serving the words. You serve yourself, too, of course, but the pleasure in serving yourself is in serving someone else as well as possible."

As a practitioner of interpretive illustration—and not merely an echo of the author, even when the author happens to be himself—Sendak has said, "You must never illustrate exactly what is written. You must find a space in the text so that pictures can do the work. Then you must let the words take over where words do it best. It's a funny kind of juggling act, which takes a lot of technique and experience to keep the rhythm going." The reader, however, should never be aware of this. "You have worked out a text so supple," the artist explains, "that it stops and goes, stops and goes, with pictures shrewdly interspersed. The pictures, too, become so supple that there's an interchangeability between them and the words; they each tell two stories at the same time. The peculiar gift in being an illustrator is that one has an odd affinity with words—it's natural to interpret them, like a composer who thinks music while reading poetry. The illustrator's first task is to comprehend deeply the nature of his text, then to give life to that comprehension in his own medium, the picture. I like to think of myself as setting words to pictures," Sendak says. "A true picture book is a visual poem."

For him, this special genre was born in nineteenth-century England with the work of Randolph Caldecott. As he sees Caldecott's contribution, "There is a juxtaposition of picture and word, a counterpoint, which never happened before. Words are left out and the picture says it. Pictures are left out and the word says it. To me, this was the invention of the picture book."

Another of Caldecott's gifts, Sendak feels, was his ability to read into things. Words and lines of verse took on unobvious meanings, colors, and dramatic qualities. "This is what the illustrator's job is all about," Sendak says, "to interpret the text as a musical conductor interprets a score."

For himself, Sendak says that he always thinks in terms of animating a text, because this is the means by which an artist entices children into a book. "There must be a breathing of life, a surging swing into action," he explains, "to have a successful illustration." The word *quicken*, he feels, best describes the spirit of picture-book animation. "It suggests a beat—a heartbeat, a musical beat, the beginning of a dance," the artist offers. "To conceive musically, for me, means to quicken the life of the illustrated book." And he has long felt that children respond most spontaneously to those illustrations with a sense of music and dance, "not something just glued onto the page."

When Sendak came to do his own picture books, he credited Caldecott with putting him where he wanted to be. "Caldecott is an illustrator, a songwriter, a choreographer, a stage manager—he is, simply, superb. He can take four lines of verse with little meaning in themselves and stretch them into a book with tremendous meaning—not overloaded, no sentimentality in it." This is exactly what Sendak did in 1965, when he took two Mother Goose rhymes and turned them into an homage to Caldecott.

Hector Protector and As I Went over the Water, his second picture book, contains a pair of inspired improvisations in the Caldecottian manner. The artist had turned to Mother Goose as a sort of trial balloon to see how he and the Old Dame got along, because he was thinking of doing a full Mother Goose collection for Harper at the time. As he once explained to a colleague, "A nursery rhyme from Mother Goose, which might have meant something quite specific in an earlier century, means nothing now. You can make of it what you will." He then cited as the perfect example:

> Hector Protector was dressed all in green
> Hector Protector was sent to the Queen.
> The Queen did not like him, no more did the King,
> So Hector Protector was sent back again.

"It's a super text—a very funny rhyme, with a lively meter and peculiar language. What's going on?—well, that's the illustrator's game. Whatever tale you tell must begin with Hector Protector dressed all in green, but he can be a boy in China, Alaska, or Israel. It's your story to do with as you please as a picture-book illustrator."

There is, of course, yet another appeal in Mother Goose rhymes—or any traditional tale, for that matter. The texts are generally in the public domain (i. e., no longer protected by copyright law) and an illustrator who uses them for book material often receives the full royalty on his or her work rather than having to divide it with an author.

Describing his approach to this ready-made text, Sendak says: "What I did was in the traditional manner of the Caldecott books. I started with one line—the first line of the verse—and then developed it in a series of pictures that just un-folded. The one line suggested material for a whole flow of images. And when I reached the end of that, the next line unraveled the next flow, and so on with the third and fourth. What I did was to invent a picture story within a four-line verse, which was great fun, because the verse itself offered no clues as to what the story should be about."

Sendak's *Hector* opens with one of his familiar, negative little heroes shouting

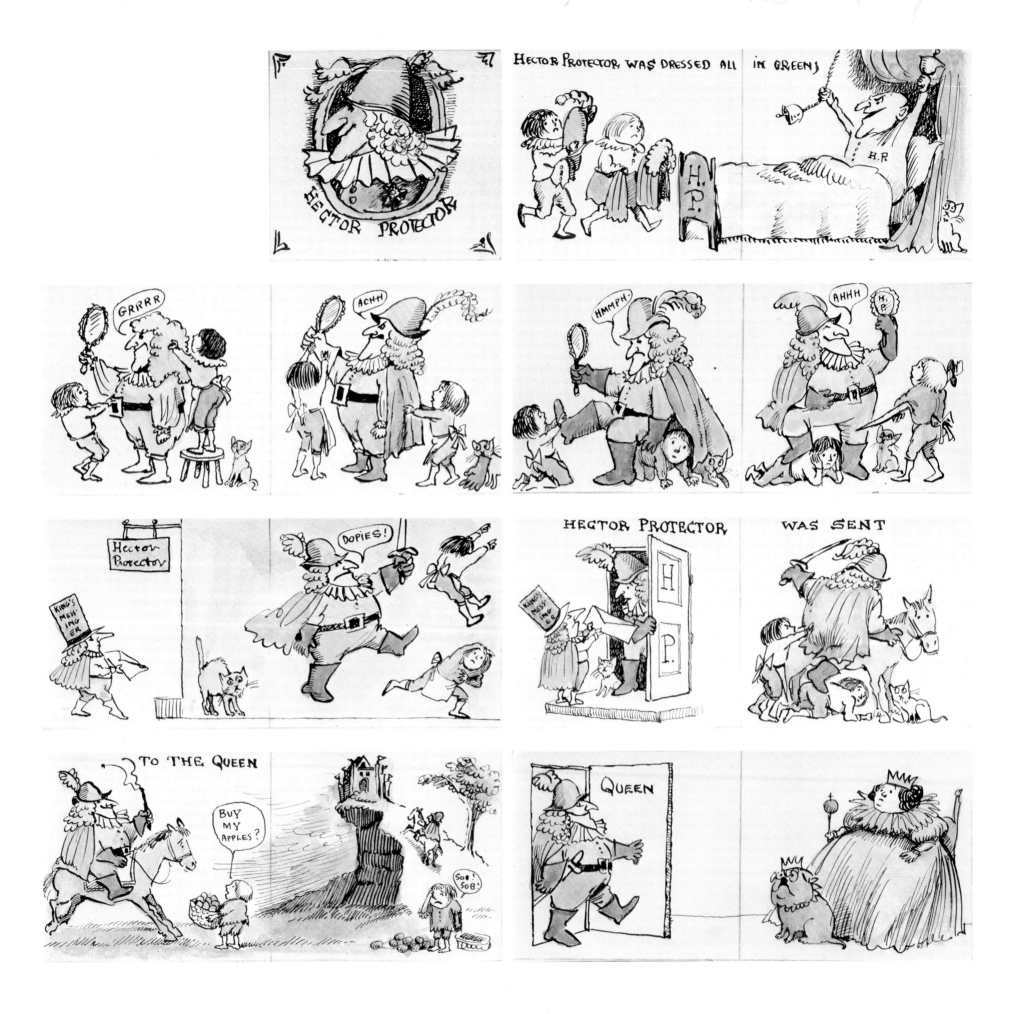

Panels from three early dummies for Hector Protector. *1964. Pen-and-ink line and watercolor.*

Panels from two working dummies for Hector Protector. *1964. Pen-and-ink line.*

"No—No No No!," as his unflappable mother tries to stuff him into a dandyish green outfit.

Though Sendak's illustrations still employ a good deal of background crosshatching, the foreground figures are painted in clear, soft watercolor tints reminiscent of comic-strip art of the 1930s. This effect is enhanced by the use of improvised bits of dialogue in comic-style balloons to help bend the verse to his own plot aims.

Outfitted like a miniature chevalier, the unwilling hero is dispatched on his mission—a pure Sendak invention—to deliver a cake baked by his mother "For Her Highness." Angry at everyone, Hector gives the boxed cake a swift kick instead, declaring, "I hate the Queen." Then, from between two trees, emerges a familiar figure: the aggressive Sendak lion, who offers a mildly menacing "Grrr-r." Arriving at the palace, mounted on the lion—and minus the cake—Hector boldly barges through a door marked "Queen's Room." Behind him skulks the Queen's coroneted dog (Sendak's Sealyham, Jennie); and before him sits none other than Queen Victoria herself, reading from *Mother Goose*. The boorish Hector is dismissed summarily by both Queen and King, and the tale's final illustrations show a disgraced young hero back home. Banished to his room (as was Max), Hector is last seen trying to cadge a piece of the undelivered cake from the blackbird who now has it. As a comic grace note, it is the bird who now shouts "No!" A closing vignette reveals the blackbird, having consumed the entire cake by himself, look-

ing as though he will live to rue his gluttony. This perfect Caldecottian touch ends a rich and cleverly sustained improvisation.

The verse's companion piece, *As I Went over the Water*, is an even less known Mother Goose rhyme:

> As I went over the water
>   the water went over me.
> I saw two little blackbirds sitting on a tree.
> One called me a rascal
>   and one called me a thief.
> I took up my little black stick
>   and knocked out all their teeth!

Not nearly as evocative as *Hector*, it may have posed more of a challenge to the illustrator. Sendak begins by providing the rhyme with a junior naval hero. This small sea captain, in charge of the good ship *Victor*, encounters an overweight (and under-scary) sea monster who swallows his vessel—all but the jaunty pennant flying from its stern. Undaunted, the young salt swims ashore to a convenient island inhabited by two rude blackbirds. Venting his anger and frustration on them, he knocks out all their teeth (as called for by the text). While this violence is taking place, the sea monster begins, in slow motion, to regurgitate the *Victor*. All ends well, with monster, blackbirds, and sea captain (his vessel recovered) forming a companionable foursome. A full-color jacket gives precisely the right weight to the book's contents; it features three of the main characters from *Hector* to one from the lesser accompanying rhyme.

Apparently intrigued by *Hector*'s open-ended possibilities for story improvisation, Sendak had done several alternate dummies, one of which depicted Hector as a middle-aged gallant with amorous designs on the Queen. Despite its bawdier charms, this version lost out to the one likelier to appeal to an audience of young children.

Surely it is relevant that Sendak always creates his pictures with music in the background. "More often than not," he says, "my instinctive choice of composer or musical form for the day has the galvanizing effect of making me conscious of my direction. I find something uncanny in the way a musical phrase, a sensuous vocal line, or a patch of Wagnerian color will clarify an entire approach or style for a new work. A favorite activity of mine is sitting in front of the record player as though possessed by a *dybbuk*, and allowing the music to provoke an automatic, stream-of-consciousness kind of drawing. Sometimes the pictures that result are

merely choreographed episodes, imagined figures dancing imagined ballets. But more interesting and useful for my work are the childhood fantasies reactivated by the music and explored uninhibitedly by my pen."

The peculiar power of music to release fantasy fascinates Sendak. "Music was the inevitable accompaniment to my childhood make-believe," he explains. "No fantasy of mine was complete without the restless, ceaseless sound of impromptu humming, the din of unconscious music-making to conjure up just the right fantastical atmosphere. The spontaneous breaking into song and dance is a natural and instinctive part of childhood. It is, perhaps, the way children best express the inexpressible. Fantasy and feeling lie beyond the words yet available to a child— and both demand a more profound, more biological expression: the primitive expression of music."

"My intention isn't to prove that music is the sole enlivening force behind the creation of pictures for children," the artist says a bit sheepishly, knowing that he is often carried away by his enthusiasms. "But music is the impulse that most stimulates my own work and I eagerly look for its presence in the work of the picture-book artists I most respect."

In reviewing a picture book by the veteran English illustrator Edward Ardizzone, Sendak once wrote admiringly, "As is usual for him, he performs like a sympathetic pianist who supports and shows to best advantage the singer he is accompanying." Of another picture book, this time one by Tomi Ungerer, Sendak

Above: from Hector Protector. *1965. Pen-and-ink line, with watercolor separations. 4¹/₁₆ x 11⁷/₁₆".* *Overleaf: from* As I Went over the Water. *1965. Pen-and-ink line, with watercolor separations. 4¹/₁₆ x 11⁷/₁₆"*

Endpaper from Hector Protector and As I Went over the Water. *1965. Pen-and-ink line, with watercolor separations. 3¾ x 8⅝"*

said, "Ungerer's pictures are blazingly beautiful, but they also keep time, never outpace, and always enlarge on his concise handful of sentences."

Looking critically at his own career, he feels that "the musical analogy is nowhere more apparent than in my earliest illustrations for Ruth Krauss's books. Her lovely and original poetry has a flexibility that allowed me the maximum space to execute my fantasy variations on a Kraussian theme, and the last page from *I'll Be You and You Be Me* is probably the simplest expression of my devotion to music. When this kind of drawing works, I feel like a magician because I am creating the air for a writer."

Sendak takes his work as a picture-book artist seriously and is often "infuriated and insulted" when his books are considered mere trifles for the nursery. "If you've worked as much as two or three years on a book, and put your life into it, you expect the point of view of the professionals to be somewhat larger, more expansive. You certainly hope the book will be read by people of all ages."

He feels that when adults, particularly librarians and teachers, review children's books, a collision inevitably occurs with their preconceptions about children. "There is a whole theory about childhood that everybody works from," he feels.

People look for whether a picture book has followed the "rules" about what is right and healthy for children. This comes into conflict all the time with those things that are mysterious, because no serious artist's work is ever just a single thing. What I object to is that picture books are judged from a particular, pedantic point of view vis-à-vis their relation to children—and I insist that any work of art is much more.

Besides, children don't need this approach to a book. They are much more catholic in taste; they'll tolerate ambiguities, peculiarities, and things illogical; they will take them into their unconscious and deal with them as best they can.

Most people are out to protect children from what they think is dangerous. Genuine artists have the same concern. Their work, however, may not conform to what the specialists think is right or wrong for children. Artists are going to put elements into their work that come from their deepest selves. They draw on a peculiar vein from their own childhoods that is always open and alive. This is their particular gift. They understand that children know a lot more than people give them credit for. Children are willing to deal with many dubious subjects that grownups think they shouldn't know about.

Children are seldom protected from terrible television, and no one protects children from life, because you cannot; and all we're trying to do in serious work is to tell them about life. What's wrong with that? You must tell the truth about a subject to a child as well as you are able, without any mitigating of that truth. You must allow that children are small, courageous people who deal every day with a multitude of problems, just as adults do, and that they are unprepared for most things. What they yearn for most is a bit of truth somewhere.

As for the criteria Sendak would bring to the judgment of picture books, he feels strongly that "originality of vision is paramount—someone who says something, even something very commonplace, in a totally original and fresh way. We shouldn't look for pyrotechnics, but for a person who thinks freshly." "For myself," he adds, "the picture book is where I put down those fantasies that have been with me all my life, and where I give them a *form* that means something. I live inside the picture book; it's where I fight all my battles, and where, hopefully, I win my wars."

To a class of his students at the Parsons School of Design, Sendak said one morning after he had been looking over the picture books they had been illustrating, and in many cases writing as well, for their semester's outside project, "Do you ever think about what you're doing? Out of chaos, you are making something real that people can respond to and love. That's the great joy of being an artist."

Inspired Pastiches

Work of the Sixties

The fame and financial security that came to Sendak following the publication of *Where the Wild Things Are*—and, more important, the seriousness with which this work was taken—gave the thirty-five-year-old artist the confidence and freedom to pursue other new directions. As he had said on accepting the Caldecott Medal for *Wild Things*: "I feel that I am at the end of a long apprenticeship. By that I mean all my previous work now seems to have been an elaborate preparation for it [*Wild Things*]. I believe it is an immense step forward for me, a critical stage in my work."

For Jan Wahl's *Pleasant Fieldmouse* (1964), a commitment undertaken before *Wild Things* was published, Sendak returned to drawings reminiscent of those he had done in the 1950s for DeJong's books. But his new illustrations are, not surprisingly, more richly realized. Not only are the various animal characters highly individualized, but background landscape—the foliage and bark of trees, the curious conformation of ferns, the contents of a milkweed pod—are all delineated with masterly ease. Even more than in the *Little Bear* books, not only an appropriate setting but also a palpable atmosphere has been created. The artist's fox—sly, treacherous, but insinuatingly charming—is the essence of woodland villainy; his mouse, wearing a bottle cap as a rakish headdress, is modestly conceived, yet immediately likeable; and the matronly hedgehog, dressed in an incongruous, frilly

Above: from Pleasant Fieldmouse. *1964. Pen-and-ink line. 4¼ x 6⅜".*
Opposite: from The Bat-Poet. *1964. Pen-and-ink line. 6⁵⁄₁₆ x 9⅝".*

nightgown, is a figure at once comic and poignant. Author Wahl's wordy tale relies more heavily on setting and character than it does on plot, and Sendak's contribution is crucial to the charm and interest of the work.

His next black-and-white illustrations, for a story by the poet Randall Jarrell, *The Bat-Poet,* further reflect Sendak's renewed interest in landscape. The frontispiece picture, a lovingly rendered forest-scape, is reminiscent of the best of nineteenth-century English engravings. His depiction of the bat family, and its one poetic offspring, is closer to meticulous nature drawing than illustration for a children's tale. It puts the viewer in mind of Beatrix Potter's exquisite animal studies. Sendak, in fact, owns a Potter watercolor of bats. The book's only double-page drawing is a moonlit landscape, revealing a mysterious lion and cub.

Of his relationship with Jarrell, Sendak says, "I've worked with many writers, but he was probably the most extraordinary of them all, because he was a poet and had a visionary sense. But, oddly for a writer, he also had a graphic sense, so that he knew what a book could look like. Yet he never tried to dictate to me what it should look like. Randall conceived of the book whole, from its binding to the quality of the paper, so working with him was an amazing experience." Though

From The Bee-Man of Orn. *1964. Pen-and-ink line and watercolor. Gatefold: 3³/₁₆ x 14³/₈". Above: 7⁷/₈ x 6¹³/₁₆"*

artist and poet met only a dozen or so times, their common interest in music and bookmaking made them immediate friends.

Jarrell came to children's books by a circuitous route. He had been asked in 1962 by a young editor at Macmillan, Michael di Capua, to translate anew four Grimm tales for a series of children's classics. The poet accepted the commission, and he so enjoyed the experience that he began to think seriously of writing a children's book of his own. Meanwhile, Di Capua was so pleased with the Jarrell translations that he began to consider commissioning a larger Grimm collection, translated by the poet and with new pictures by a major American illustrator. Having recently seen Sendak's *Nutshell Library*, as well as the artist's illustrations for the three German tales translated by Doris Orgel, Di Capua felt that Sendak would be a perfect illustrator for Grimm. While he and Sendak were discussing the prospect of a lavish Grimm in full color, Jarrell's story *The Bat-Poet* arrived at Macmillan. Di Capua immediately asked Sendak to illustrate it.

"When the pictures for *The Bat-Poet* were finished," Sendak remembers, "it was remarkable, because as Jarrell and I looked over the illustrations together, there were images in the art which he had never discussed with me; images which appeared as though we had picked each other's brains. There was, for example, a drawing of a lion at the end of the book, though no lion is mentioned in the poem at all. Jarrell was greatly startled; not only was the lion his special favorite beast, it had been the image that evoked the poem originally. He hadn't transmitted this fact to me in any way, yet the lion was there. To me, this was one of those unique moments in a collaboration."

Sendak's only pictures in color during 1964 were done for a second Frank Stockton story, *The Bee-Man of Orn*. Freer in spirit than those in *The Griffin and the Minor Canon*, they also paid more attention to background—lovingly detailed trees, fences, streams, and farmhouses—again confirming the artist's renewed interest in setting. The influence of two nineteenth-century English mentors is clearly discernible: Caldecott and the earlier watercolorist/caricaturist Thomas Rowlandson. The story is about a contented beekeeper whose life is disrupted by the appearance of a young sorcerer who tells him that he has been "transformed." The Bee-Man cannot rest until he discovers what it is he has been transformed *from*. When the answer turns out to be a baby, the beekeeper makes a wish to return to his former state. He is granted the wish, only to grow up, once more, to be the contented Bee-Man of Orn. How the Bee-Man manages to rescue a screaming infant from the grasp of a Ghastly Griffin comprises the tale's moment of highest suspense. The squalling babe, one of many inspired babies to appear in Sendak works from this time on, is rendered comically, yet with genuine affection.

Probably the book's most memorable illustration is the one in which the distinctly unhandsome Bee-Man is changed back into a baby. Except for its size and the disappearance of a characteristic stubble, his face, ludicrously peering out from under a baby bonnet, is unchanged.

In 1965, Sendak did the illustrations for *Lullabies and Night Songs*, a large-format, seventy-two-page song book edited by William Engvick, with music by Alec Wilder. The four-color artwork bears a close stylistic resemblance to that of *Hector Protector*, light in overall spirit and pale of palette, but with the crosshatching all but eliminated. The illustrations have a directness and clarity appropriate to a book aimed at the youngest listeners. The songs are a mix of traditional melodies and lyrics, as arranged by Wilder, and original melodies written by him for a

Following pages: from Lullabies and Night Songs. *1965. Pen-and-ink line and watercolor. "The Golux's Song" title: 1 x 7¼". "The Golux's Song" illustration: 4½ x 7¼". "The Huntsmen": 6 x 7¼"*

 # THE GOLUX'S SONG

variety of well- and lesser-known poems (from William Blake, Robert Louis Stevenson, Mother Goose, James Thurber, and others). Many of the pictures reflect Sendak's admiration for his favorite nineteenth-century artists, among them Blake, George Cruikshank, Samuel Palmer, and Thomas Rowlandson. Other illustrations range stylistically from comic-strip art to lyrical landscape decorations. "The Christ Child's Lullaby," and "Evening Is a Little Boy." Sendak's Sealyham, Jennie, plays several parts in the work, from walk-on roles in many of the charming, inch-high title decorations to the heroine in "Rock-A-Bye, Baby." She is the comic relief in "Bobbie Shaftoe," where she can be seen shamelessly eating the fruit off a grand lady's beribboned bonnet.

The same year he did *Lullabies and Night Songs*, Sendak illustrated a second book by Randall Jarrell, *The Animal Family*. He had refused on a first reading to consider doing the artwork. "It seemed to me impossible and dangerous," he recalls. "There are certain books I cannot illustrate, books which in my opinion should never be illustrated. This was one of them, because the images were so personal and so graphically created in the writing that Jarrell didn't need me. We discussed the book together, and he still wanted something of my contribution, though he believed what I said. So we decided not to illustrate the book but to decorate it—which is, in fact, the word we did use. Rather than try to depict anything specific, I thought of his book almost as if each chapter represented a different theatrical setting. These settings were my personal landscapes of what Jarrell was talking about. There is nothing animate in them. Some readers claim to see animals and other creatures, even people, but nothing of the kind is there. They are simply black-and-white landscape settings for each chapter of the book."

These highly romantic scenes are of trees, rocks, and water. In one there appears a house; in another a canoe. The set piece for the chapter titled "The Bear" is perhaps the most evocative, bathed as it is in an eerie light which falls on both foliage and rocks. Stared at for any length of time, the rocks on the left begin to look like draperies, and one can imagine a bearlike figure on the right.

A second way in which this particular work was illustrated had to do with design. The book is about family: not having, and then having, a family on an island. Sendak and Jarrell decided to place the text in small, contained blocks at the center of each page. "The words would then look like a tight little island," Sendak explained, "surrounded by extremely wide, white margins, representing the world outside. The squarish, fat shape of the book itself became the family's little house." The plan of the work, beautifully executed by the artist's favorite children's book designer, Atha Tehon, thus comprised a major part of its decoration.

It was in Isaac Bashevis Singer's *Zlateh the Goat and Other Stories*, published in

Opposite: chapter decoration from The Animal Family. *1965. Pen-and-ink line. 5⅛ x 3⅞"*

1966, that Sendak's illustration took a new and promising direction. For this collection of seven tales steeped in Jewish folklore, he decided to use photographs of his own relatives from the Old Country. "All those dead Jews in my family—those who died in Hitler's holocaust, or after lives of hardship and deprivation, had always been very close and important to me." And so the artist took particular faces and costumes from old, worn family photographs and transformed them into Singer's characters with a precision and finality that are hauntingly memorable. In the story "Fool's Paradise," the hero, Atzel, modeled after Sendak's maternal grandfather, lies in bed, an uncannily otherworldly look on his face (he thinks he is dead and now in heaven). The figure of the Devil in "Grandmother's Tale" is among the most inventive and commanding of the illustrations. He is the perfect graphic incarnation of Singer's lines: "He rose with a loud laugh, stuck his tongue out to his belly and grew twice as tall. Horns came from behind his ears, and there he stood, a devil." His existence cannot be doubted, because there he is, cloven-hooved, in an absolutely authentic East European cap, wearing unquestionably real knickers, vest, and coat, and towering over an undeniably real menorah (the nine-branched candelabrum used to commemorate Hanukah). The dwarf-figures who dance in the foreground with the *dreidel* (a four-sided top which is a traditional Hanukah plaything) would later exert a marked influence on Sendak's illustration for the Grimm tale "The Goblins." For "The Mixed-Up Feet of the Silly Bridegroom," the artist highlights the faces of three of his heroines, as if by spotlight, with marked photographic effect. In "The First Schlemiel," the old man is adapted from a photograph of a relative. The disgruntled baby in the same story is a figure the artist would use with increasing frequency, often basing it on photographs of himself as an infant.

In 1967, Sendak did drawings for George MacDonald's *The Golden Key*. It was a labor of love, because Sendak admired MacDonald as "probably the greatest of the Victorian writers for children." What he particularly liked was the author's ability to work on the reader at different levels of feeling. MacDonald could tell a conventional fairy tale with all the ingredients a satisfactory fairy tale required and, at the same time, imbue his stories with a kind of dream-magic arising from his own unconscious. *The Golden Key* is one of MacDonald's most mysterious tales. Its hero and heroine, Mossy and Tangle, are children when the story begins and an old couple about to die at the tale's end. The substance of the narrative concerns their adventures in and beyond fairyland, as Mossy seeks a door into which his golden key will fit. Though Sendak's black-and-white illustrations here are not based on photographs, several of them have the same quality of super-realism that characterizes the artwork in *Zlateh the Goat*. (The picture of Tangle caught in a web

Opposite: from "Grandmother's Tale," in Zlateh the Goat and Other Stories. *1966. Pen-and-ink line. 6³⁄₈ x 4"*

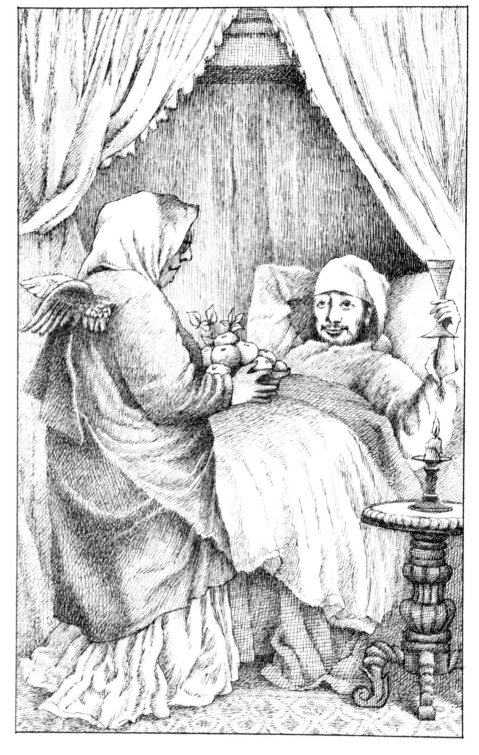

*Left: from "The First Schlemiel" and right, from
"Fool's Paradise," in* Zlateh the Goat and Other
Stories. *1966. Pen-and-ink line. Each 6⅜" x 4"*

From The Golden Key. *1967. Pen-and-ink line.*
Each 5³⁄₁₆ x 3¹⁄₄″

of encircling tree branches is one example.) If there is a fault in the illustrations, it is that they somehow lack consistency of style and overall authority. It is as though they were done by two different people. The difficulty lies in part with the tale itself, which begins in the real world, but moves progressively deeper into an ethereal realm inhabited by specter-like figures. It appears not to be a realm in which the artist was entirely at home—or possibly this book, like Jarrell's *The Animal Family*, does not lend itself to illustration.

In 1967, too, one of Sendak's most evocative drawings was published for a memorial volume to Randall Jarrell: an illustration for Jarrell's poem "Children Selecting Books in a Library" (see page 6). The figure of a somber child is taken exactly from a Sendak family photograph of the artist's mother with the three Sendak children. Here, the artist extracts his brother, Jack. The fanciful ogre in the background is Sendak's own invention, gaining credence from the real child, room, and dog that share the pictorial space with him. Other elements add to the illustration's internal magic: a full moon shining outside; leafy tree branches growing within the library; book shelves blending mysteriously into the window curtain behind the boy's head.

Probably no single book provides more dramatic evidence of the changes that were taking place during the sixties in Sendak, and in his work, than the fifth and final *Little Bear* book, *A Kiss for Little Bear,* which appeared in 1968. There had been a seven-year hiatus since the fourth book, *Little Bear's Visit,* and it is doubtful that the fifth volume would have come into being at all had Sendak not suffered a serious heart attack in the spring of 1967. The shock of hearing this news from Ursula Nordstrom served as a spur to author Else Minarik. She had long been thinking about writing a fifth book in the series, but it was her painful realization that Little Bear might never again come to life via Sendak's pen that brought a sense of urgency to the project. The manuscript of *A Kiss for Little Bear* reached Harper early in the fall of 1967; it was the only book that Sendak illustrated during the year he took off for recovery. "I was so frightened I'd never work again that the book was like a crutch," he remembers gratefully. Before he even began its drawings, he confided to a friend, "I feel my work has permanently changed tone, color, and meaning, without my yet having put pen to paper. I am as curious about me as though I were someone else."

Unlike any of its predecessors, each of which were more than sixty pages long, the final book had only thirty-two pages and it contained a single tale rather than a quartet of stories. A curious sort of valentine from Minarik to Sendak, the book is about Little Bear as artist. He draws a picture—a small bear's version of a wild thing—and sends it as a gift to his grandmother, via Hen. On receiving it,

Grandmother dispatches a proxy kiss to Little Bear, which is passed from Hen to Frog to Cat to boy Skunk to girl Skunk, and, eventually, to its rightful recipient. Many adult readers have been shocked to see how much Grandmother Bear has aged since last encountered. Dressed in a somber Victorian costume complete with ruffled cap, she looks more like Whistler's grandmother than Little Bear's. The artist seems unable to temper his observations to suit the slightness of the tale. There is an overworked and brooding—almost ominous—quality to much of the drawing. Yet this coda to the series contains some of the tenderest illustrations of Sendak's career. Many of the pictorial details give the impression of having been lingered over lovingly—each blade of grass, the bristles of Little Bear's fur, the ripples on Cat's sleek back. They are rendered with near-obsessive care, almost with an invalid's hypersensitivity to the world's heartbreaking beauty. The work closes with the wedding of the two skunks, an occasion to bring together all the characters from all the previous *Little Bear* books—including Little Bear's only human-being friend, Emily, and her doll Lucy. So subdued and elegiac is the tone of the nuptial gathering that it could be taken for a funeral, were it not for the Japanese lanterns suspended above the guests' heads. (Even so, there is a frog who looks as though he is about to strangle himself on the line from which they hang.) There is no doubt in the reader's mind that this is a curtain call for the entire cast—and for the most successful series of easy readers in our time.

In 1969, a slimmer Sendak, fully recovered, illustrated a second George MacDonald fairy tale, *The Light Princess*, a narrative far more accessible to today's readers than *The Golden Key*. It is the story of a baby princess cursed at her christening by a disgruntled guest: she is deprived of her gravity. Not only is the princess unfailingly cheerful and given to fits of laughter at inappropriate moments, she is also without weight: "The slightest gust of wind would blow her away." The artist's frontispiece illustration of the nude infant princess, floating in the air like a helium-filled balloon outside her unsuspecting mother's window, sets the magical tone of the tale. An observant viewer will note the presence of a slight breeze in the motion of a tassel on the window shade, and in the wondrous suggestion of movement in the gauzy curtain behind the Queen's head. The frontal nudity of this royal girl-child brought Sendak none of the outraged letters that came his way a year later when a nude little boy appeared in his own picture book *In the Night Kitchen*. At the climax of the MacDonald tale, the intensely-felt illustration of the now-grown heroine, looking over the side of her boat at the drowning prince who loves her (and who has the face of Sendak himself, though the artist was unaware of the resemblance when he drew the picture), is hypnotically compelling. It is the moment of truth: the princess must overcome her levity or lose

Following pages: from A Kiss for Little Bear. 1968. Pen-and-ink line, with three color separations. Left: 6⅛ x 5¼". Right: 5¹⁵⁄₁₆ x 5"

Opposite: frontispiece from
The Light Princess.
1969. Pen-and-ink line.
5¹/₁₆ x 3³/₁₆"

her beloved. The significance of the occasion is almost religious in feeling, the illustration itself a sort of last communion. Though the oar of the princess's barque seems awkwardly drawn, it works beautifully to emphasize the separation between hero and heroine.

It is Sendak's black-and-white work that changes most dramatically during the sixties. Not only is his draftsmanship notably surer and the pictorial content richer, but his style is exquisitely responsive to the work at hand. Thus, a slight tale like Jan Wahl's *Pleasant Fieldmouse* is bolstered by the artist's fanciful characterizations and well-defined forest setting. Texts as strong as Jarrell's *The Bat-Poet* and *The Animal Family* are accompanied by reticent graphics, more like background music than operatic scores. For an equally strong text in the folklore tradition, however, Singer's *Zlateh the Goat,* Sendak felt that documentary-style illustrations could make a dramatic contribution, and he successfully injected figures from his own Jewish past into the author's Old World fables. That Sendak so effectively achieves his artistic goals without either upstaging or being out of tune with the author's words is high tribute to his deepening talent. Even in works where his success was par-tial—as in *The Golden Key*—the illustrations are always interesting.

In color, too, the artist was moving toward greater subtlety and simplification. His *Bee-Man of Orn* has a refreshing spontaneity, his *Hector Protector* is an admira-bly clever synchronization of existing text with improvised pictorial accompani-ment. As for *Lullabies and Night Songs,* there is a new subtlety and sophistication in the palette, a return to reliance on line rather than modeling that suggests his later flat, comic-book style in *In the Night Kitchen.* As the decade drew to a close, Sendak's entire repertoire was more reflective of his own developing interests and taste. The mature artist was emerging.

Jennie

"The Love of My Life"

Opposite: from Higglety Pigglety Pop!. *1967. Pen-and-ink line. 2¾" high. Above: sketch for* Higglety Pigglety Pop!. *1966. Pen-and-ink line. 1⅞ x 2⅜"*

The year 1967 was probably the worst of Sendak's life. During May, on a trip to England, the artist suffered a major coronary attack and, for the first time as an adult, was deeply shaken by intimations of his own mortality. "I was amazed. I couldn't believe it was happening—that my mission could be cut short like that. I felt as though a bargain had been broken, that so long as I kept working and honestly recalling my childhood, I had been granted some sort of immunity."

What happened was that Sendak had arrived in Newcastle-upon-Tyne with his English editor, Judy Taylor of The Bodley Head publishing house. He was to be interviewed that night on BBC-TV, and then, the following day, they planned to visit the birthplace of Thomas Bewick, the eighteenth-century master engraver. The BBC program was well under way when Sendak began to feel sick and suddenly found that he couldn't speak. Somehow or other the televised conversation was brought to a close, the BBC interviewer gave Sendak some whiskey, and the artist and Miss Taylor returned to their hotel. Sendak went to bed, but was too uncomfortable to sleep. His journal entry that night read "I think I'm dying." Finally, a doctor was summoned and gave the reassuring diagnosis of severe indigestion. But Judy Taylor remained uneasy. She had a friend who had recently suffered a heart attack, and so she insisted on calling an ambulance, which took Sendak to the hospital. Her suspicion was confirmed. "If it weren't for Judy," Sendak says, "I most likely wouldn't be here now."

He was taken to Queen Elizabeth Hospital in Gateshead-upon-Tyne, the best place in the area for cardiac care. There, among the great many get-well cards he received, was a homemade one from Tomi Ungerer. It featured a pop-up nurse hidden ingeniously in the invalid's bedcovers. While recuperating, the artist arranged for a friend to send postcards home to his parents from different places in Europe. His mother was suffering from cancer, and he did not want to add to her burdens. "What good would it have done to have told my mother about my heart attack before she died?" he asks.

After five weeks, Sendak was moved to a nursing home in London, which visitors could reach more easily. The illustrator Edward Ardizzone, who became a cherished friend, was a frequent caller. "Ted taught me how to take snuff, so I wouldn't miss cigarettes as much," he recalls fondly, "though I don't think the staff approved of a cardiac patient sneezing his head off." Sendak was released from the nursing home on his thirty-ninth birthday. Before leaving England, the artist promised to provide The Bodley Head with seven small sepia drawings for a private printing of selected poems from William Blake's *Songs of Innocence*. He ultimately presented the originals to Judy Taylor, to whom he felt he owed his life.

Above left: detail from Mrs. Piggle-Wiggle's Farm. *1954. Pen-and-ink line. 2½ x 2¼". Above right: from* Circus Girl. *1957. Pen-and-ink line, with three wash separations. 4½ x 4⅝". Opposite: from* What Do You Say, Dear?. *1958. Pen-and-ink line, with two wash separations. 6⅞ x 16½"*

The illustrations included a lion, a lamb, a nude angel, a bearded old man, and a little boy crying (to accompany "The Echoing Green"). For Sendak, this last-mentioned drawing "sums up that whole awful time to me." To this day he doesn't like to look at any of the Blake illustrations because they bring back too many unhappy memories.

No sooner had Sendak returned to the United States when he discovered that his beloved Sealyham, Jennie, had cancer, too. He decided to spend the summer resting on Fire Island and took Jennie with him, determined to make her better. "Meanwhile," Sendak remembers, "my mother had a relapse, and they didn't tell me, because they were afraid I would have a relapse. Finally they told me, and I didn't want to go see her. I sat there for a week. I just couldn't face it. Eventually I went. And I came back to Jennie. It was all a nightmare, but Jennie never complained. She wasn't a complaining dog. Then I asked my friend Gene Glynn to take her over to Bay Shore and have her put away." The following week, Sendak wrote an old acquaintance, "My best friend, my dog Jennie, has died." The artist's mother died a year later, in August 1968.

Sendak had been preoccupied for more than a year with the unhappy possibility of Jennie's dying. *Higglety Pigglety Pop! or There Must Be More to Life*, his tribute to Jennie, was published in the fall of 1967, scarcely a month after the dog's death. As Sendak says: "I wrote it when Jennie was getting old, and I was afraid she was going to die. Somehow it was easier to work up an anxiety about the dog's dying than about my mother, because that was just too much to go for. Then, when the book was finished, I went to England and had my coronary." Early in September, when Sendak received his first copies of *Higglety Pigglety Pop!*, he wept.

Sendak was, of course, not the first author/artist to immortalize a beloved pet. Beatrix Potter, in the privately printed edition of *The Tale of Peter Rabbit*, wrote on the flyleaf of her own copy: "In affectionate remembrance of poor old Peter Rabbit, who died on the 26th of January 1901, at the end of his ninth year. He was bought, at a very tender age, in the Uxbridge Road for the exorbitant sum of 4/6. Whatever the limitations of his intellect or the outward shortcomings of his fur, and his ears and toes, his disposition was uniformly amiable and his temper unfailingly sweet. An affectionate companion and a good friend." It is entirely possible that Peter, too, had, a few months before his death, grown noticeably old and infirm, and that this circumstance provided the impetus Beatrix Potter needed to write to her former governess's son, Noel Moore, requesting that the child return on loan the tale that she had so lightly spun for him in a letter of 1893. She had for some time been thinking of reworking it for publication.

Jennie had appeared regularly in almost every one of the artist's works from 1954 on. After a first bit part in Betty MacDonald's *Mrs. Piggle-Wiggle's Farm*, she played roles in *What Do You Do, Dear?* and *What Do You Say, Dear?*, as well as *Chicken Soup with Rice, One Was Johnny*, and many other books. Her most exalted part was as Queen Victoria's dog in *Hector Protector*—she had her very own crown—but her best-known appearance surely was in *Where the Wild Things Are*, in which she is the initial victim of young Max's wild behavior: he chases her down the stairs. It is, however, in *Higglety Pigglety Pop! or There Must Be More to Life*, her *prima donna assoluta* farewell bow, that the Sealyham bids for immortality.

Who was this dog of many parts? Jennie was born in Killingworth, Connecticut, during the summer of 1953. Sendak was then twenty-five and, in his own words, "desperately in need of a dog." As he remembers it, "A friend had told me about two kind ladies in Killingworth who bred Sealyham terriers and were eager to rid themselves of a runt. They were even willing to give her away. That was in August 1953, and I had Jennie in New York about twelve weeks later." Two days before she was scheduled to arrive in the city, Sendak did a series of fantasy drawings about a baby who turns into a dog. These proved to be prophetic of Sendak's

Opposite: fantasy sequence predating Jennie's arrival. 1953. Pen-and-ink line. 10 x 7⅜"

IT'S A DOG'S LIFE

BAHHHH -HIC-

TAP- TAP-

BOO

HOOO HOOO

BOOO-HOO! -TOUGH!

M. Sendak nov. '53

fourteen-year relationship with Jennie. She was baby, child, companion, and best friend. "Jennie was the love of my life," he says unabashedly.

"Jennie un-runted quickly," Sendak boasts, "and some months later I proudly brought her back to Killingworth to show her off to her breeders and her own very fashionable mama and papa. The two ladies were delighted. They had named her Mona Lisa, but she became Jennie to me shortly thereafter." Four years later, when Jennie returned to Killingworth to stay with her breeders while Sendak spent a month in Italy, they wrote to him extolling Jennie's "charms and mischievousness." It was a letter Sendak cherished until Jennie died, but then it made him "too sad" to reread.

Of Jennie's memorial volume, his major prose work to date, Sendak says, "*Higglety Pigglety Pop!* is the longest book I've ever written [sixty-nine pages]. There's much in it from my own life."

An intriguing and decidedly American fairy tale, *Higglety* begins where the traditional Old World tale leaves off: at "And they lived happily ever after." Its dog heroine has everything—a loving master, two windows from which to enjoy the view, two pillows ("a round pillow upstairs and a square pillow downstairs"), two bowls to eat from—in short, all the comforts any reasonable animal could covet in this life. Yet the story opens on Jennie's packing her leather bag and beating a hasty retreat from this seemingly idyllic existence. "I am discontented," she announces. "I want something I do not have. There must be more to life than having everything."

On leaving home, Jennie answers an advertisement for a leading lady in the World Mother Goose Theatre. Told that she needs experience, she takes a job as a nursemaid to an angry, unpleasant baby (a definite reversal of roles with her real-life master who often served as *her* nursemaid). When Jennie bravely rescues Baby from the jaws of the menacing Downstairs Lion—putting her own life in jeopardy—she is at last welcomed as the leading lady.

Jennie's starring role for the book's grand finale is in the Mother Goose Theatre's rendition of an American nursery rhyme written by Samuel Griswold Goodrich in 1846:

> Higglety Pigglety Pop!
> The dog has eaten the mop!
> The pig's in a hurry.
> The cat's in a flurry.
> Higglety Pigglety Pop!

In the end, Jennie once more has "everything," but it is a different sort of everything from the wealth of material comforts in which she wallowed at the book's start. The dog has now proven herself in the world of art outside her master's home and has found fulfillment by fully utilizing her twin talents for acting and eating. Only once does "the finest leading lady the World Mother Goose Theatre ever had" remember her old master and send him a letter:

> Hello,
> As you probably noticed, I went away forever. I am very experienced now and very famous. I am even a star. Every day I eat a mop, twice on Saturday. It is made of salami and that is my favorite. I get plenty to drink too, so don't worry. I can't tell you how to get to the Castle Yonder because I don't know where it is. But if ever you come this way, look for me.
>
> Jennie

Frontispiece from Higglety Pigglety Pop!, *with
its related snapshot. 1967. Pen-and-ink line.*
4³/₈ x 4⁹/₁₆"

Illustration from Higglety Pigglety Pop!, *with its related snapshot. 1967. Pen-and-ink line.*
$4^3/_8 \times 4^9/_{16}''$

Though there are moments of high comedy (mostly concerned with Jennie's shameless gourmandizing), *Higglety Pigglety Pop!* is essentially a melancholy tale, reflecting as it does Sendak's forebodings about Jennie's and his mother's deaths. Castle Yonder, Jennie's final destination, is Sendak's perfect childlike metaphor for heaven—or what an artist's heaven might be like. Refreshingly absent from *Higglety* is the element of predictability. The reader has little idea of how it will all turn out until the last page is turned.

Sendak wanted his pet's final appearance to be a no-holds-barred Jennie Spectacular, something that would immortalize her in the World Mother Goose Theatre— i.e., the realm of children's books—where her master was playing an increasingly important role. Not only is Jennie, the work's central character, an alter ego of Sendak's, but the all-important supporting player, Baby, is also Sendak himself, taken almost exactly from that crucial family-album photograph of Sadie Sendak with the three Sendak children. The fact that Baby is ultimately magically transformed into Mother Goose (who, in the illustration, bears more than a fleeting resemblance to Sadie) is perhaps symbolic of Sendak's concern with his own mortality, and his hope of living on through his work. As a winner of the Caldecott Medal and the leading American children's book artist of his time, Sendak might reasonably hope to join Mother Goose as one of the immortals of children's literature.

Thinly disguised bits of autobiography abound. (Of more than passing interest is the fact that in *Higglety* Baby has been abandoned by his parents, a situation anticipated by his creator, whose mother was ill with cancer, and whose father was old.) The malcontent canine heroine's fated destination is "a big white house outside of town." Sendak himself was, at the time, interested in finding a country house. A few years later—almost as if Jennie's fictional destination were a mirror image of his own—he bought a handsome, old "big white house outside of town" in Ridgefield, Connecticut. (Curiously enough, the house has yet another *Higglety, Pigglety, Pop!* association. Samuel Griswold Goodrich, author of the title rhyme, was born in Ridgefield.) And, in the course of her travels, Jennie engages in philosophical discourse with an ash tree, during which she complains, "You have everything—you are taller than I am." Sendak has often referred to himself, partly in jest, but partly with the remembered pain of being one of the shortest boys in his high school class, as "a dwarf." Possibly one of his bonds with Jennie was the fact that she was among the smaller breeds of dog.

Is there a particular significance in the enigmatic route to immortality taken by Sendak's canine heroine? She wins her place in the World Mother Goose The-

160

atre only after successfully doing battle with the lion who is about to devour Baby. If we take this awesome Downstairs Lion character as representing aggression and destructiveness, then what Jennie effects is nothing less than the rescue of Baby from his own rage and negative impulses. Is this not exactly what the author/artist himself tries to achieve in the work of his lifetime? By accepting and exploring the angers and cares, the fears and joys of small children, Sendak helps to release them from constricting emotional bondage of various kinds.

Once questioned by a reader as to why Jennie doesn't return to her master at the end of the book—Does this mean that she had died?—Sendak replied, "Essentially, yes, but Jennie in real life would abandon her owner if the food was not good—or if the food elsewhere were better."

From Higglety Pigglety
Pop!. *1967. Pen-and-ink
line. 4⅜ x 4⁹∕₁₆″*

As for the nursery-rhyme drama itself, Sendak was dealing with a verse as opaque as "Hector Protector." It had been composed by its author, an advocate of factual works for children, in the misguided belief that a verse so patently absurd would, once and for all, laugh the frivolous old Goose lady right off the American literary stage. It was up to Sendak to transform the nonsense rhyme into whatever he chose. Though we have no inkling of it as Sendak's story unfolds, each of the characters in his prose fantasy will return as a supporting player in the World Mother Goose Theatre's production of "Higglety." Rhoda, the downstairs maid in Baby's house, narrates Jennie's verse saga; the pig, who wears a sandwich board and dispenses tasty snacks early in the book, comes back in the nursery rhyme to be "in a hurry"; the cat milkman acts out "in a flurry"; while Sendak's Downstairs

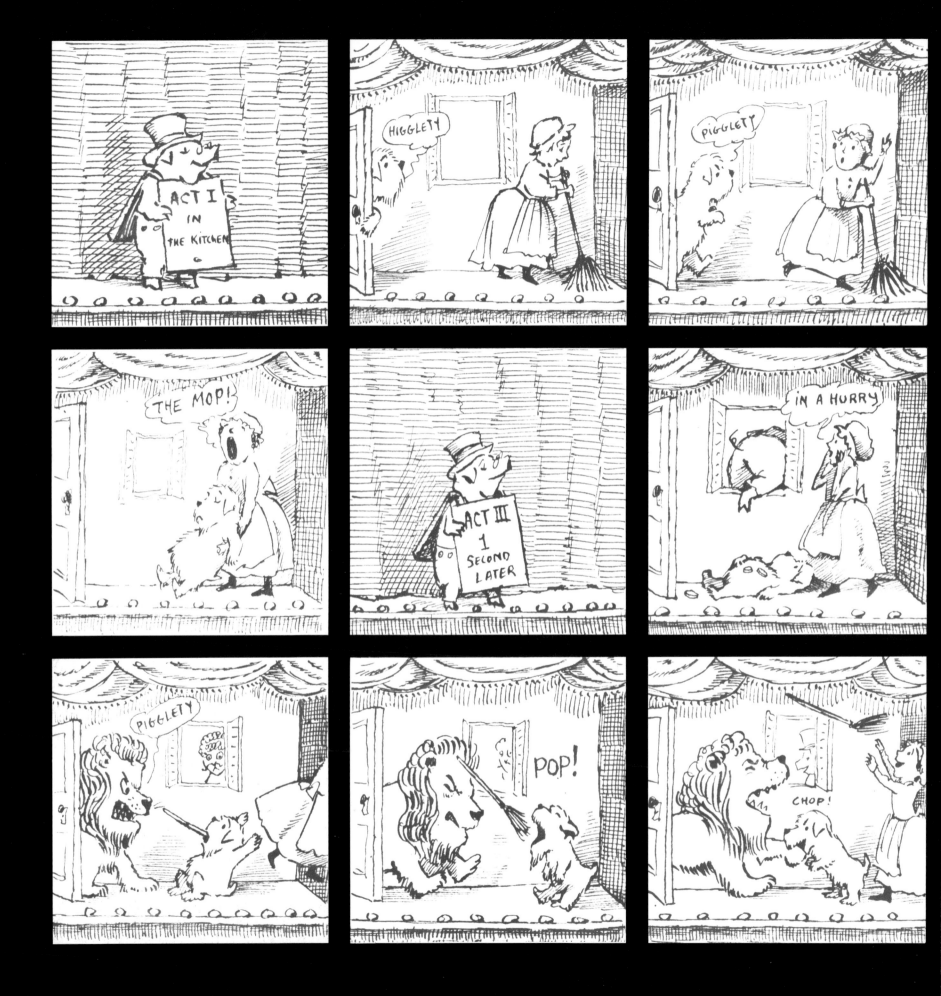

The World Mother Goose Theatre production, from **Higglety Pigglety Pop!**. *1967. Pen-and-ink line. Each frame 4³⁄₈ x 4⁹⁄₁₆"*

artist's memory of the wooden horse and Borden milk wagon his Aunt Esther gave him as a child. "The toy wagon had little tin milk trays inside and real little glass bottles that clinked together when you removed them," he recalls. "There was also a little wooden driver." Sendak has said that without this particular toy, none of his books would ever have been written, an indication that the milk wagon had doubtless been his own vehicle for transporting himself to "someplace else where I'd rather be." (Not without relevance in a book so concerned with death and immortality is the fact that, for a long time, Sendak had also played with the big box the toy had come in. He used to climb inside it and close its lid—as if it were a coffin. Possibly the milk wagon is associated with a hearse in the artist's mind, good reason for its place in this somber work.) Though his own toy milk wagon had long since disappeared, Sendak received a letter from a woman who had read *Higglety Pigglety Pop!* and recognized the wagon. She generously sent the artist her own duplicate of the very toy he had long been searching for.

The circular emblem at the book's close—of Jennie holding her mop made of salami—is a graphic summation of the heroine's achievement of true bliss. Not only is she the leading lady in the World Mother Goose Theatre, but she is also able to satisfy her insatiable appetite by swallowing a salami mop every day—"twice on Saturday." Surely Jennie is destined to live happily forever in the hereafter, a new twist to the traditional fairy-tale ending. As Sendak says, "In her future life, I think of Jennie as being an actress, always eating a mop and performing that idiotic little nursery rhyme forever in some kind of artist's heaven where you can continue to work."

When he returned to the city from Fire Island at the end of the summer of 1967, the artist told a friend, "When I'm stronger I shall 'start' another puppy. I long for a golden retriever, though everyone tells me it is cruel to keep one in the city." Yet, more than a year later he wrote to someone inquiring about whether or not he was still interested in the breed, "I am suddenly sadly hesitant about my retriever. I still dream of Jennie, and the pain is unrelenting."

It was not until the artist moved to Ridgefield in 1972 that he was able to face the prospect of a replacement for Jennie. He got a female golden retriever, whom he named Io, and soon afterward a German shepherd he called Erda. Later, when Erda had puppies, he kept the only surviving male and named him Agamemnon. It was almost as if loyalty to Jennie would not allow him ever to become attached to just one dog again.

Opposite: from Higglety Pigglety Pop!. *1967. Pen-and-ink line. 4³/₈ x 4⁹/₁₆"*

In the Night Kitchen

A Picture Book "From the Direct Middle of Me"

Opposite: half-title page from In the Night Kitchen. *1970. Pen-and-ink line, with watercolor separations. Diameter: 5⁵⁄₁₆".*
Above: from dummy for In the Night Kitchen. *1969. Pen-and-ink line and watercolor. ⅞ x 1¹¹⁄₁₆"*

For some time, Sendak had been thinking about gathering a congenial selection of traditional nursery rhymes and setting them to pictures. As he remembers it, "I began a Mother Goose collection in 1969 by putting together some of my favorite verses, but I soon noticed that—typical of me—they all had to do with eating. I wasn't conscious of it, but I had collected rhymes about bakeries and stews and cooking pots, and I realized that I was doing a cookbook or something else other than Mother Goose." That something else turned out to be the most joyous picture book of his career to date, *In the Night Kitchen.*

As it happened, this work made good use of some of the verses he had chosen for the abandoned Mother Goose project. His hero Mickey's triumphal pronouncement "I'm in the milk and the milk's in me" is a variation of the rhyme "I see the moon, / And the moon sees me; / God bless the moon / And God bless me." Assuredly, the plot itself was influenced by another of the verses Sendak had selected and had already made a first sketch of: "Blow, wind, blow / And go, mill, go! / That the miller may grind his corn; / That the baker may take it, / And into bread make it, / And bring us a loaf in the morn." Sendak's preliminary drawing

173

BABY AND I

WERE BAKED IN A PIE. THE GRAVY WAS WONDERFUL HOT.

WE HAD NOTHING TO PAY TO THE BAKER THAT DAY

AND SO WE CREPT OUT OF THE POT.

for this latter verse contained a small hero in a bed very like Mickey's in *Night Kitchen* and a single baker similar in size and shape to the trio who came to dominate the Night Kitchen.

The artist has revealed yet another aspect of *In the Night Kitchen*'s derivation: "When I was a child," Sendak explains, "there was an advertisement which I remember very clearly. It was for the Sunshine Bakers, and the advertisement read 'We Bake While You Sleep!' This seemed to me the most sadistic thing in the world, because all I wanted to do was stay up and watch. And it was so arbitrary and cruel of them to do it while I slept. Also, for them to think I would think that was terrific on their part, you know, and would eat their product on top of that! It bothered me a good deal, and I remember I used to save the coupons showing the three fat little Sunshine bakers going off to this magic place, wherever it was, at night to have their fun, while I had to go to bed. This book was a sort of vendetta book," the artist confesses, "to get back at them and to let them know that I was now old enough to stay up at night and know what was happening in the Night Kitchen."

Between these various ingredients and the final picture book lies the secret of Sendak's genius. When he had completed his text for *Night Kitchen* in the spring of 1969, he confided to an old friend, "I have written a new picture-book text, and I'm mad for it—and *it's* mad. I feel so sure of it, something not common for me. It comes from the direct middle of me, and it hurt like hell extracting it. Yes, indeed, very birth-delivery type pains, and it's about as regressed as I imagine I can go. Simply, it's divine. I leave for Europe July 24th—home September 17th—and then

Mother Goose sequences, for a proposed nursery rhyme collection. 1969. Pen-and-ink line. Above: 1⅞ x 6½". Opposite: 2⅛ x 5½"

BLOW, WIND BLOW! AND GO, MILL GO! THAT THE MILLER MAY GRIND HIS CORN;

THAT THE BAKER MAY TAKE IT, AND INTO BREAD BAKE IT,

AND BRING US A LOAF IN THE MORN.

I plow into the illustrations. I will hate that, because it's going to be very hard!" Sendak's gradually increasing pleasure in what he himself has written is evident, and the metaphor of giving birth to a book is one that he would use again and again.

On his return from abroad, the artist began making journal notes for the pictures in *Night Kitchen*. An entry for September 27, 1969, reads, "Style very simple à la Meggendorfer [a late nineteenth-century illustrator of toy books]. Series of moving panels—too comic-bookish? Maybe. Spreads must vary in exciting fashion—like a film. Fast!" On another occasion, he wrote, "The wish to animate a book is always there." The ultimate comic-book-art simplicity of the *In the Night Kitchen* illustrations doubtless owes most to an exhibition that Sendak saw some two years after the publication of *Where the Wild Things Are*. The Metropolitan Museum of Art had an exhibit of pages from *Little Nemo in Slumberland*, Winsor McCay's famous newspaper comic strip which ran from 1905 to 1911. Before the show, Sendak had been unaware of this popular American artist's genius for graphic fantasy. "It now sent me scooting back, with new eyes, to the popular art of my own childhood," he recalls.

Like Sendak's first book, *Kenny's Window*, the theme of *In the Night Kitchen* is a dream, in this instance a happy one that poses few problems for its hero, and asks nothing of its audience beyond the willingness to surrender to its own irrepressible dream logic. A small boy, Mickey, is wakened by a racket in the night and falls through the dark, out of his pajamas, past his sleeping parents' bedroom, and into a bowl of dough in the moon-and-star-lit Night Kitchen. Here, three identical

Working dummy sketches for In the Night Kitchen. *1969. Pen-and-ink line and watercolor. Top left: 15/16 x 1 11/16". Bottom left: 2 1/8 x 2 1/16". Top right: 2 1/8 x 2 1/16". Bottom right: 2 1/8 x 2 1/8". Opposite: from* In the Night Kitchen. *1970. Pen-and-ink line, with watercolor separations. 6 7/8 x 7 1/4"*

AND FELL THROUGH THE DARK, OUT OF HIS CLOTHES

bakers absentmindedly mix Mickey into their batter "so we can have cake in the morn." Mickey manages to escape being baked and flies over the Night Kitchen's Milky Way in an airplane fashioned out of bread dough. Once aloft, he procures a crucial cup of milk for the bakers and then, triumphant, slides down the side of the milk bottle and back into his own bed. "And that's why," the story ends slap-happily, "thanks to Mickey we have cake every morning."

In the first small dummy for *In the Night Kitchen*, the final mise-en-scène is not at all developed. There is no hint of the elaborate setting the Night Kitchen

Above: early sequence for In the Night Kitchen. *1969. Pen-and-ink line. 11 x 8½". Opposite: early sketches for* In the Night Kitchen. *1969. Pen-and-ink line. 11 x 8½"*

178

will ultimately have, with its box, carton, and jar skyscrapers fancifully topped by a variety of cooking utensils; there are no Oliver Hardy triplets as bakers and no marvelously nostalgic thirties furnishings. In fact, Sendak at one point considered picturing the bakers as three animals. It proved to be an old Laurel and Hardy movie rerun on TV—*Nothing but Trouble*—that gave him the inspiration to cast a trio of Hardy look-alikes as bakers in his book. The first dummy's purpose was simply to lay out the picture-book dream logically. "And there were serious problems," Sendak recalls. "I had to get Mickey from bed, down to the kitchen, up to

Overleaf: from In the Night Kitchen. *1970. Pen-and-ink line, with watercolor separations. 10⅛ x 16⅛"*

the sky, into the milk bottle, down from the milk bottle, and back into his bed. It was just a lumbering, difficult job getting that kid to budge." Essentially, it is the illustrator's layout that must help to transport his characters from one place to another. As Sendak sees it, "This becomes the unconscious shaping of the book. What's interesting is that I always do the initial dummy fairly quickly, and then I go into the study drawings where I correct if something is wrong with my layout. But I hardly ever have to correct the overall scheme. Which means that the first instinctual thing is right." (Nonetheless, because of the particular difficulties in making its dream-logic plausible, *In the Night Kitchen* required four different dummies.) Once Sendak has solved all his technical problems, he does his final drawings on tracing paper. This is easily erasable, and the finished art is readily transferable (by using a light box) to the high-quality paper on which the completed artwork is submitted to the publisher.

By the time the final, full-color illustrations were completed, Sendak had turned *In the Night Kitchen* into a near cinematic tribute—a quasi-Busby Berkeley musical extravaganza—to his own thirties childhood in New York. The artist pays scrupulous attention to authentic period details within what, on the face of it, looks to be a broad, comic-book style of illustration. The small hero Mickey falls past a twenties Art Deco chandelier, and then by an immediately recognizable console model of a thirties radio (Jennie's name is clearly inscribed on the clock face above the radio) and a pair of marvelously fringed, gossamer curtains so palpably real that just seeing them on the page is like recovering a bit of the past. Mickey's destination, the Night Kitchen, is one of Sendak's richest graphic inventions: the city of New York transformed into a surreal kitchen-furnished skyline.

Aside from background details accessible to all, *In the Night Kitchen* abounds in unobtrusive private references to the artist's own life. In the first picture inside the Night Kitchen, for example, there is a bottle labeled "Kneitel's Fandango." Kenny Kneitel, a collector of, and dealer in, Mickey Mouse figures and other nostalgia items from the 1930s, had sold Sendak some of his most treasured objects. On the pages following, "Woody's Salt" refers to the late Woody Gelman, editor of the Nostalgia Press and a close friend. One of the trio of Oliver Hardy bakers pours from a flour sack with a memorial label for Jennie which reads: "1953. Jennie. 1967 Bay Shore, L.I." A highly unlikely container for shortening (a cloth sack) carries the name of Jennie's birthplace, "Killingworth, Connecticut." A giant cream container lists two happy addresses from the artist's peripatetic Brooklyn childhood: "1717 West 6th St." and "1756 58th St." (Actually, this cardboard cream container is of a sort that did not exist in the thirties, but the shape suited Sendak, and he elected to use it.) Some pages later, there is a carton labeled "Eugene's" and another container with the legend "Philip's best tomatoes." Eugene is the close friend who took Jennie to Bay Shore to be put out of her misery, and Philip is the artist's father. A companion container of tomato paste on the same page is labeled "Sadie's best," a reference to the artist's mother. Still farther on, the inscription on a coconut carton reads, "Patented June 10th 1928," the artist's birthdate; a stop on the elevated train reads "Jennie Street"; and yet another carton is labeled "Schickel," a reference to the writer Richard Schickel, whose biography of Walt Disney prodded Sendak's memory about his childhood love of Mickey Mouse and his youthful admiration for Mickey's creator. There are several other private references, the final one being to "Q. E. Gateshead," the hospital in England where Sendak recovered from his heart attack.

The wordless center spread of the book is mesmerizing, with its midnight-blue sky dotted with stars, its bread-loaf train, and its various boxes, bottles, cartons, and sacks forming an awesome mock-architectural replica of the great metropolis. Largest of all, in the foreground, is the all-important milk bottle from which Mickey must wrest the vitally needed cup of milk. (In an early dummy, Mickey climbs up the side of the bottle and exits via an unlikely door at its base.)

The spread of the three bakers chanting the refrain "Milk in the batter! Milk in the batter! We bake cake! And nothing's the matter" is again a fully animated scene. One baker employs his mixing spoon as a mandolin, another shouts through a funnel as if it were a megaphone, the third holds his spoon like a microphone. There is a definite musical beat, and one can almost sense the bakers bursting into an impromptu dance as they chant. A smiling, self-satisfied Mickey sits atop the milk bottle in the distance, his mission accomplished.

The climactic "Cock-a-doodle Doo!" illustration reveals Mickey triumphant, milk pitcher perched jauntily on his head, crowing at the dawn and his impending return to the waking world. The emblem of Mickey on the half-title page, which repeats itself, with only a change in background, on the book's closing page, is somehow reminiscent of the grinning Mickey Mouse of thirties films.

The style of the art throughout *Night Kitchen* is flat, the colors bold in their contrasts, with a decided debt to the American turn-of-the-century cartoonist Winsor McCay. There is also a debt, in the book's spectacular central spread as well as its overall ambiance, to Busby Berkeley's film *Gold Diggers of 1935*. Above all, *In the Night Kitchen* is the artist's tribute to the sensual pleasures of childhood (the physical sensations of warmth and cold, of kneading dough, of falling and flying); the sights and smells of the kitchen; and the drama and excitement of nocturnal New York.

"*In the Night Kitchen* was influenced," says Sendak, "not by an artistic mode of

the past that I considered superior [as were several earlier books done in homage to various nineteenth-century-English master illustrators], but by art that was very real and potent to a child growing up in America in the thirties and forties. *Night Kitchen* and, to a lesser degree, *Wild Things*, reflect a popular American art both crass and oddly surrealistic, an art that encompasses the Empire State Building, syncopated Disney cartoons, and aluminum-clad, comic-book heroes—an Art Moderne whose richness of detail was most sensuously catalogued in the movies." What Caldecott was to *Hector Protector*, King Kong is to *Wild Things*. What the Victorian illustrators were to *Higglety Pigglety Pop!*, Busby Berkeley and Mickey Mouse are to *Night Kitchen*. This is an oversimplification, of course, but also the truth.

Soon after *In the Night Kitchen* was published, Sendak further considered the eclectic influences on his art. "Over the years," he said, "I've been feeding myself a diet of cultural things—Blake, the English illustrators, Melville—but those crappy toys and tinsel movies of the thirties are certainly much more directly involved with my life than William Blake ever was—although Blake is unquestionably important, my cornerstone in many ways. Nobody before him ever told me that childhood was such a damned serious business. . . . But this other stuff now, it was the only art I grew up with. It's what made me . . . those movies and Mickey Mouse. And I love them! I love them!"

Where the Wild Things Are had troubled some educators and librarians because of its possibly scary monsters and open acknowledgment of a child's anger against his mother. But an even greater number of adult readers were disturbed by *In the Night Kitchen*'s candid acceptance of a young child's sexuality and the fact that its hero, Mickey, is unclothed for a good part of the story. As one New York critic saw it, "The naked hero wallows in dough, swims in milk, and otherwise disports himself in a manner that some might interpret as a masturbatory fantasy. . . . Sendak is dealing with a child's sexual feelings and he will doubtless offend those who are unprepared to acknowledge such feelings." A German critic thought he had discovered something entirely different in the work: a revelation of the Jewish artist's fear of the Nazis as a child growing up in the 1930s. To him, Mickey's dough outfit represented a suit of army fatigues (as worn by doughboys) and the Night Kitchen's "Mickey Oven" a stand-in for the Nazi crematoria. Yet another critic found the book far more upsetting than *Where the Wild Things Are*: "It is true that Mickey survives any danger that threatens," she admitted, "but surely the possibility of being baked in a cake is more disturbing than any wild creature." Beyond such individualistic interpretations and reservations, many librarians simply objected to the frontal nudity of the small hero—several going so far as to

provide him with a painted-on diaper in their libraries' copies of the book. In his interview with *Rolling Stone* magazine Sendak said, "Librarians objected to *Night Kitchen* because the boy is nude. They told me you can't have a penis in a book for children; it frightens them. Yet parents take their children to museums where they see Roman statues with their dicks broken off. You'd think that would frighten them more. But 'Art' is somehow desexualized in people's minds. My God, that would make the great artists vomit.

"In a nursery school courtyard in Switzerland," the artist continued, "there was a statue of a nude boy running. It was anatomically correct except for the genitals, which were a bronze blur. The children were upset by this; their parents complained, and the genitals were carved in. In this country it would be the other way round—we prefer the blur, the fig leaf, the diaper."

Though Sendak personally favors *In the Night Kitchen* over *Where the Wild Things Are* ("It goes so much more beneath the surface of things," he feels), the book has never achieved the spectacular popularity either of his *Nutshell Library* or *Wild Things*. However, when compared with other successful contemporary picture books, its sales figures more than hold their own. Perhaps its less wide appeal has to do with the fact that its message, for child or adult, speaks not to the reasoning mind, and this causes uneasiness. Mickey the pilot's maiden flight over the Milky Way heralds a pioneering acknowledgment in a picture book for young children of the reality and urgency of their dream lives, a reality and urgency as important as and, in some ways, more important than those of their waking lives. Perhaps none of us sufficiently values the dreams of childhood—our own or our children's. As one of the rare beings who has never lost touch with the child he once was, Sendak has given his audience a bona fide child's dream, curiously unmonitored by Maurice the adult.

Opposite: from In the Night Kitchen. *1970. Pen-and-ink line, with watercolor separations. 6⅞ x 7⅛"*

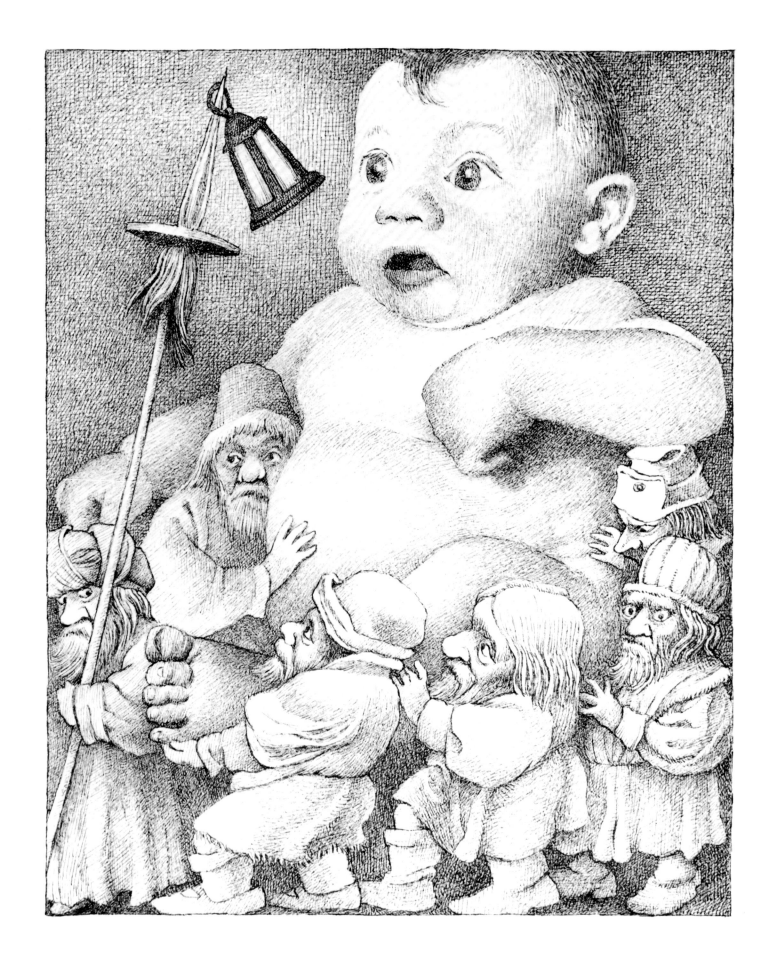

Grimm Purpose

Sendak was first approached about illustrating a new edition of selected Grimms' fairy tales in 1962. The poet Randall Jarrell had just completed four pellucid translations—"The Fisherman and His Wife," "The Golden Bird," "Hansel and Gretel," and "Snow White and the Seven Dwarfs" for a series of children's classics to be published by Macmillan. The series' editor, Michael di Capua, had the inspired idea of pairing Sendak with Grimm and Jarrell in a more ambitious contemporary American collection of the *Household Tales.* Jarrell's death in 1965 brought to a halt all plans for the project, but in 1968 the Austrian-born novelist and children's book author Lore Segal agreed to provide new translations for an indeterminate number of tales which she and Sendak were to select from Wilhelm and Jacob Grimm's complete repertoire of more than two hundred. By this time, Di Capua was an editor at Farrar, Straus and Giroux, which house ultimately published the work.

Sendak had been eager to illustrate a major collection of classic tales for some time. He had long been dissatisfied with the pictures he had done in 1959 for *Seven Tales* by Hans Christian Andersen, feeling them to be lackluster and superficial. "They were pastiches of Gothic architecture and atmosphere, which clung too closely to their models. I had not digested my experience of Europe sufficiently to turn it into something else. Probably I was too young and a little afraid of Andersen as well." Sendak was not much more pleased with his curiously subdued black-

Opposite: frontispiece from The Juniper Tree and Other Tales from Grimm. *1973. Pen-and-ink line. 4½ x 3⅝". Above: detail from "The Poor Miller's Boy and the Little Cat," in* The Juniper Tree and Other Tales from Grimm. *1973. Pen-and-ink line. 1⁷⁄₁₆ x 1⅛"*

and-white illustrations for an abbreviated children's edition, in 1963, of Leo Tolstoy's *Nikolenka's Childhood*. In Sendak's view, this effort, again, bore little fruit,
adding nothing to the work that Tolstoy's writing had not already achieved.

By contrast, from the start of the Grimm project, Sendak's enthusiasm was
unqualified and unflagging. He was older, and more experienced; he was not
intimidated by the challenge of this wide variety of tales, some as familiar as a
friend's face; others strange and quirky—comic, cruel, enigmatic, or just plain
frightening. To Sendak, the stories chosen were "the best. They have absolutely
everything: magic, wish-fulfillment, bloodcurdling horror, consuming passion—
the works. The material is remarkably rich and deep, like good soil."

Sendak and Segal each read all the Grimm tales and made separate lists of
those stories they felt must be included and others they thought worth considering. (Though Sendak had never studied German, his understanding of Yiddish
and his familiarity with a great many German lieder and opera scores enabled him
to read the language with some ease.) When they compared lists, they reserved for
further scrutiny all stories that appeared on the "consideration" lists of both, along
with those on each one's must list. On first winnowing, artist and translator were
left with seventy-five stories; these were finally pared down to the twenty-seven
that both agreed spoke most eloquently to our times. Though the number of tales
selected was small, it was decided to issue the collection in two volumes so that the
size of the typeface could be large enough to give a feeling of easy accessibility.
Di Capua points out that "the contents page itself comprises a fascinating critical
judgment." Above all, the selections reflect the taste of two sophisticated adults
choosing those tales richest in resonance for themselves. There is no attempt to
tame Grimm for an audience of children.

In 1970, when the artist began seriously to think about his drawings for the collection, which was to be called *The Juniper Tree* after one of the most moving and
elaborate of the tales, he was forty-two. As an illustrator, he had reached full
maturity. Whatever stylistic influences had been borrowed from English and conti-
nental sources were by now smoothly integrated into his work, made to serve his
own psychological insights and graphic intentions. The commanding suite of illustrations he had done in 1966 for Isaac Bashevis Singer's collection of East European tales, *Zlateh the Goat*, enabled him to say with quiet assurance, "My forte lies
in interpretive illustration, in the opening up of lines. I fight against the merely
illustrative and have no interest in it at this point in my career. There's no fun in
just setting a picture down anymore." With the Grimm tales, Sendak gave himself

the delicate and exacting task of "catching that moment when the tension between story line and emotion is at its greatest, so that the person reading is in for a surprise if he thinks it's just a simple-minded fairy tale."

With his usual meticulousness, Sendak began by seeking out the best source material. From the New York antiquarian children's book dealer Justin Schiller he was able to buy a copy of the Grimms' own three-volume 1819–22 popular second edition of *Kinder- und Hausmärchen*. He wanted to own it, so that he could experience the look, the heft, the shape, and the feel of the originals—much as he had instinctively experienced his first "real book," *The Prince and the Pauper*, as a child. As soon as the final list of tales was agreed upon, Sendak started looking seriously at the work of other major illustrators of Grimm. There was Ludwig Grimm, the younger brother of Wilhelm and Jacob, who provided a portrait of Frau Katherina Viehmann (one of the best and most prolific of the Grimms' storytelling sources) for the enlarged second edition, as well as other effective illustrations for a later collection of selected Grimm tales. And there was George Cruikshank, whose illustrations were the first to appear in an English-language version of the tales and were greatly admired by the Brothers Grimm themselves. Walter Crane, too, provided intelligent and handsomely decorative illustrations for a later edition of the tales, as did several other artists, chiefly German.

To prepare himself more fully for this long-anticipated chef-d'oeuvre, Sendak sailed to Europe on the *Raffaello* in late May of 1971—his destination: Germany. Sendak intended to visit each of the German regions from which the Grimms had gathered their tales; to stop, too, at the Grimm Museum in Kassel, and to steep himself in the landscape and language of the tales, so that his illustrations would not only be meaningful to himself and a contemporary English-language audience, but also reflective of the long tradition of Grimm. "I didn't want to project just an American, 1970s point of view," he recalls.

Like many artists who carefully arrange and control their working environments, Sendak has always been wary of travel, suffering acute anxiety attacks and premonitions of disaster or death on the eve of each long-planned departure. But his Atlantic crossing could not have been more auspicious. Sendak had taken along Herman Melville's novel *Redburn*, an early work he found to be "so youthful, so bittersweet, the very best of Melville," that it helped to induce a mood of light-hearted optimism in him as well. He also had the pleasure of having as a shipmate the music critic and author Herbert Weinstock, and the two carried on animated conversations about the language of music, about Rossini and Verdi, Mahler, and, of course, Mozart—Sendak's favorite composer. From Naples, the artist proceeded to Rome, where he embarked on "a fabulously beautiful train ride" to Zurich

Cover decoration and Welsh landscape, from Sendak's Grimm notebook. 1971. Left: pen-and-ink line. 6⅛ x 4⅛". Right: pencil. 6 x 4"

through the late-spring landscape of Umbria and Tuscany. "I must be crazy leaving for Switzerland so soon," he wrote in his diary on May 28. But plans had long been made with his German-language publisher, Daniel Keel of Diogenes Verlag, and his wife Anna: the trio would travel by car from Zurich, via Munich, into the heart of Grimm country. En route, Sendak kept a running account of daily happenings in a notebook appropriately titled "Grimm Reise." As he explains it, "*Reise*

194

is a powerful German word signifying both a physical and an emotional journey."

On June 2, the Keels and Sendak visited Munich's great Alte Pinakothek, where the artist admired both "the marvelous Dürers" and "the wondrous work of Albrecht Altdorfer, with great gushes of trees at the top of his canvasses and small people below." Sendak confessed to being bored by Brueghel. Later that day, in a Munich antique shop, he found a Grimm edition he had long been looking for, one illustrated by a nineteenth-century German little known outside his own country, Hermann Vogel.

An entry for June 3 notes briefly, "Altdorfer and Grünewald have turned me violently on to my Grimm. I begin to sketch." Three days later, he arrived in the city of Kassel in the Hesse region, where a great many of the brothers' best tales were gathered. Kassel proved a great disappointment, particularly after the small town of Berching, which Sendak had the day before pronounced "the best place so far. Take note of trees and roofs for Grimm." Kassel's Grimm Museum contained little the artist was not already familiar with, and, despairing of discovering anything fresh about the Grimms there, he spent most of his time looking at Rembrandts in the city's art museum.

As the travelers moved north toward the Heide region and Hamburg, Sendak found more to please him. In Karlshafen, on June 7, he wrote, "Slept in a Sleeping Beauty castle. Walked in the most wonderfully beautiful Reinhardswold woods. *Super Grimm!* A cuckoo called all the way. Saw caged den of wild boars. . . . Sketched in the woods next day." From Karlshafen, the party crossed the Hartz Mountains into Goslar, a place that delighted Sendak. "Caldecott was here!" he wrote with pleasure. "It is a splendid city, never bombed, with superb architecture. Bulging, burgher buildings." (Sendak would use Goslar as the setting for "The Story of One Who Set Out to Study Fear.") "The postcards I'm picking up en route," the artist noted, "will probably serve me best for Grimm, what with their accurate views of architectural detail and costume." One postcard, a reproduction of Jean-Baptiste Greuze's painting *Indolence,* provided the inspiration for Sendak's illustration for the story "Frederick and His Katelizabeth." After seven more days of mostly non-Grimm sightseeing, the trio made a slight detour in order to stop at Colmar, in Alsace, so that Sendak could see Grünewald's great Isenheim Altarpiece. "It moves me beyond words," he wrote. "His 'Resurrection' and Dürer's 'Passion' equal *The Juniper Tree.* A little Grünewald plus a lot of Dürer. I am drunk with Grünewald and a little homesick."

After driving through the Black Forest, the travelers returned to Zurich on June 21, whence Sendak flew to England. There he had arranged to meet Gene Glynn, with whom he would spend a much-needed month of rest in a Welsh cottage belonging to Ann Durell, children's book editor at E. P. Dutton. He planned to sort out his various impressions of Germany and Grimm country.

Once settled in Wales, Sendak began to think about the composition of an illustration for one of the tales, "Hans My Hedgehog." "Include clumps of various greens behind Tintern Abbey," he told himself, making a rough sketch. Considering the project as a whole, Sendak noted, "Also try for combination views of terror and beauty." He alludes here to a convention employed by various Renaissance artists, who, in their narrative paintings, often combined idyllic background landscapes—viewed through small arches or porticos—with dominant foreground subject matter that was terrible and gory. "Use Wales for cheerfulness, Germany for gloom," Sendak wrote in his diary. But, aside from a few perfunctory entries about "Rabbit's Bride" and "Hansel and Gretel," Sendak contented himself with sketching the Welsh landscape. His pencil drawings of the countryside around Veddw are as tenderly observed and full of feeling as his early sketches of children. The artist did refer to a more personal event on July 7, 1971: "Began to grow beard." Perhaps he felt the need to give himself a graver demeanor commensurate with the high seriousness of the Grimm assignment he was about to begin. On the other hand, he later wrote a friend, "The trip was marvelous—all of it—I was so happy I even grew a beard."

For Sendak, working on the Grimm pictures coincided in many ways with his settling comfortably into middle age. Everything in his life seemed to be falling into place. In February 1972, when he was just finishing the tenth Grimm drawing—for "Rapunzel"—the artist bought a cooperative apartment on lower Fifth Avenue. About the same time, Sendak realized his long-cherished dream and bought what he refers to, only partly in jest, as "my *goyishe* Franchot Tone house" in Ridgefield, Connecticut. He was delighted with the sprawling structure, part of it dating back to the eighteenth century, and its resemblance to the country houses used as posh settings in the movies he had seen as a child. City-born and bred, however, Sendak found the transition to country squiredom difficult—even mildly frightening. He was made uneasy by the unfamiliarity of country noises—so much more varied than city traffic sounds. The first Grimm drawing he did in his new country house—an illustration for "Fitcher's Feathered Bird"—reflected his general malaise. "In the background is a country villa with skulls instead of plants on all the window ledges, and there are bits of limbs lying in the soil. I was projecting my own feeling about the scariness of living in the country that first year," he admits. "The facts of the Grimm story dovetailed with those of my own life, without my doing violence to the illustrator's role."

By the time Sendak returned to New York from his German pilgrimage, he had decided that the only three illustrated Grimms he really liked were those by George Cruikshank (1823), Ludwig Grimm (1819 and on), and Otto Ubbelohde (1905). "They are all robust, outward Grimms, steering clear of anything murky or deep," he says admiringly. Sendak's interpretation, too, would offer a robust, if more intellectualized and inward Grimm. Almost all his pictures have a dark and brooding atmosphere: an earthy, primitive—occasionally almost cruel—quality. They are not easily forgotten.

During August and September of 1971, before actually beginning to draw, Sendak reread all twenty-seven of the Grimm stories, making marginal notes for himself. These notes usually included the artist's underscoring of what he felt to be the crucial sentence of a given tale. For "The Frog King, or Iron Henry," he underlined, "But when she was lying in bed, he came crawling and said, 'I'm tired, too, and want to sleep just as comfortably as you.'" A comment on "The Fisherman and His Wife" reads, "No fish! No hut! No palace! Her à la Grafina Potatska! Yes!" Questioned about this last reference, Sendak laughs and explains that his mother, when angry, often referred to his father as "Graf Potatska." "Potatska was apparently a dimwitted Polish count who just sat around issuing orders, without ever thinking of the consequences." The facial expression that ultimately found its way into the illustration of the insatiably ambitious wife was "definitely my mother's," Sendak says.

Once ready to illustrate, Sendak made several decisions influenced by his admiration for Dürer's *Little Passion*, a compact set of thirty-six woodcuts based on the life of Christ, which he describes as "brimful of graphic marvels." At first, he had planned to do a chastely decorative Grimm, one in which each story would have headpiece and tailpiece—as in Walter Crane's illustrations—as well as a single major drawing; but, inspired by the power of the Dürer work, Sendak opted for a monkish simplicity. There are no distracting page decorations or graphic furbelows anywhere in the book. His single illustrations, one for each tale, are almost exactly the size of Dürer's etchings for *The Little Passion*, and their densely worked, crosshatched backgrounds are more reminiscent of etching than drawing. Sendak greatly admired Dürer's "highly wrought finishedness, his figures bursting out of the borders." In *The Juniper Tree* the same device is used with great boldness and psychological impact. Sendak's pictures, almost suffocatingly claustrophobic, seem to force their way out of their small rectangular enclosures, thereby imposing their alien reality on the viewer. The close focus makes for a brutal assault on the imagination. In much the same way that a Diane Arbus photograph almost violates the viewer, Sendak thrusts his vision of the tales upon us. These decidedly virile Grimm illustrations can neither be denied nor dismissed.

The first illustration for the Grimm volumes was begun on December 27, 1971, some six months after Sendak's return from Germany, and the last picture was completed fifteen months later, on March 4, 1973. To appreciate fully the magnitude of Sendak's accomplishment—the artist's loving attention to myriad details of dress, gesture, mood, setting, and expression; the breadth of his visual references; the wholehearted care with which he considered each picture's content and composition for maximum impact on the reader—one must examine each drawing closely. It is rewarding as well to study some of the visual changes and refinements that occurred between many of the first sketches and their final illustrations. In four instances, in fact, the artist discarded his initial conception entirely and took a fresh tack.

Sendak's illustration for "The Three Feathers" required seven days from rough sketch to finished illustration. One of the artist's early drawings, it worked right from the start. "The cap on the toad's head is taken from Dürer's Pontius Pilate," he says. As the sketch was refined into the sure outlines of the final picture, the toad grew dramatically bigger. Though Sendak feels the illustration works well, he is not totally satisfied with it: "It skirts the merely illustrative by too narrow a margin."

The drawing for "The Devil and His Three Golden Hairs" took five days. The figure of the Devil's grandmother is a portrait of Katherina Viehmann, the teller of this tale and of "The Three Feathers," "Frederick and His Katelizabeth," "The Poor Miller's Boy and the Cat," and "Hans My Hedgehog" of those tales se-

Left: from "The Devil and His Three Golden Hairs," in The Juniper Tree and Other Tales from Grimm. *1973. Pen-and-ink line. 4½ x 3⅝". Above: Katherina Viehmann, frontispiece engraving by Ludwig Grimm for the enlarged second edition of* Kinder-und Hausmärchen. *1819*

Left: the rejected finished drawing and right, the published version from "Snow White and the Seven Dwarfs," in The Juniper Tree and Other Tales from Grimm. *1973. Pen-and-ink line. Each 4½ x 3⅝"*

lected for *The Juniper Tree*. Sendak took the old storyteller's face and figure directly from Ludwig Grimm's frontispiece engraving for the second edition of the tales. She is the traditional frontispiece drawing for all German editions of Grimm to this day, and it was her posture that determined Sendak's composition. "It's a highly erotic and disturbingly ambiguous drawing," the artist feels, "with the Devil lying awkwardly and suggestively in the old woman's lap." The Devil's secret is divulged in what Sendak calls a background "balloon."

The illustration for "Snow White and the Seven Dwarfs" was begun on October 22, 1972. Redone twice, it was finished early in March 1973, the last drawing to be completed for the collection. The more familiar the tale, Sendak discovered, the more difficult it was to find just the right moment to illustrate. After trying two versions of Snow White with the dwarfs—several dwarfs in one sketch, just two in another—Sendak decided that the tension of the story really revolved around the older generation—represented by the Queen—trying to keep the younger one—personified by Snow White—in its place. The Queen, consulting her mirror, is the tale's central figure because she is the cleverest. "The whole composition is a vision," Sendak says. "I put it together and used it for all it was worth." This said, the artist admits to being almost equally fond of his discarded illustration of Snow White with just two dwarfs.

Between the start of the picture for "Rabbit's Bride" on November 20, 1972, and its completion nine days later, an old and close friend of Sendak died. Perhaps the intense melancholy of Rabbit's expression owes something to this sad event. "The story is very slight," Sendak feels, "but luckily it stops at just that charged moment of intense suffering, when the rabbit discovers his love has gone and left him holding a bag of worthless sticks."

The illustration for "Hansel and Gretel" required more than two weeks. Again, it proved difficult because of the tale's familiarity. "From my own life," Sendak says, "I took Erda, my beautiful German shepherd, and got her into the act to guard the children against the witch. The composition was borrowed from Ludwig Grimm. I made up the witch in no time at all, but Gretel is pretty in a way I had never attempted before in my drawings of children. I was determined that she be both beautiful and thoroughly brave. I've caught her the very second before she performs her fearless deed and becomes a *mensch* [a grown-up, responsible person]. What is so sad in 'Hansel and Gretel,' of course, is the father's passive acquiescence in letting his children die."

The illustration for "The Master Thief" was also done in two versions and took the artist some six weeks to complete. Sendak describes the final drawing as "pure Fuseli in composition." (Henry Fuseli was a Swiss-English artist of the late eighteenth century, an admirer and contemporary of William Blake, with a surreal imagination and a strain of eroticism in much of his work.) Of the picture's content, Sendak explains, "It's a child's primal fantasy, my own, actually, and too private to go into, but the elements suited both me and the tale. When you don't have such personal components blended in, you're just illustrating. . . . This highly complex composition somehow came easily. I guess the easy ones are those already in your head."

For "The Fisherman and His Wife," as Sendak's marginal note indicated, he strove to find a previously unillustrated but pivotal line. He lit on "The sun was about to rise, and as she saw the red of the dawn, she sat up in bed and stared straight out into it." On a personal level, the drawing is an homage to Sendak's

golden retriever Io as a puppy. She sits contentedly on the bed, apparently a favorite resting place for baby Io. "The fisherman's wife is desperately my mother," Sendak says, "but both Grünewald and Fuseli inspired the composition. The wife's headdress comes directly from a Fuseli. Most Grimm men are completely dominated by their women, as in this story, which I do not much like. It hasn't the quickness, directness, or happy weirdness of many of the others."

The commanding frontispiece drawing for volume 1 of *The Juniper Tree* is, in Sendak's estimation, "perhaps the single most successful drawing in the book." Finished in less than a week, it illustrates a brief but haunting Grimm tale about goblins who steal a baby away from its unsuspecting mother, leaving a changeling in its place. This particular illustration is related both to the drawing of the Devil with its dwarf-figures in *Zlateh the Goat* and to the picture of the baby who sits on the floor in the story "The First Shlemiel" in the same work. There is also a close kinship to the illustrations of Baby in *Higglety Pigglety Pop!* "Though the baby here is essentially me," Sendak says, "the toes, the heft, and something of the strange mood come out of a curious German photographic album I picked up on one of my trips abroad."

Describing "The Goblins" illustration to an audience at Harvard College, Sendak said, "I did a picture of a human baby being carried off by goblins. It was lovingly depicted because I love to draw babies. Given any opportunity, I draw them. But the picture is confusing. Someone wrote me, 'I'm very puzzled. I like it a lot, but the expression on the child's face is so idiotic. Could you tell me—is this the changeling or the real baby?' And I realized that I honestly didn't know. Because if you watch a normal, healthy baby, it *is* somewhat idiotic looking—no offense meant to newborn babies. They dribble in much the same way as one imagines a changeling would." This very ambiguity, of course, accounts for the picture's grip on the viewer.

One of the last Grimm illustrations completed was the drawing for "The Two Journeymen," a brutal and frightening depiction of the tale's adversaries, tailor and cobbler. Sendak is pleased with "the gorgeous composition out of Dürer's *Little Passion* and with its English pre-Raphaelite overtones. The picture, showing one man's cruel conquest of another, befits this chilling tale of good and evil. The principals loom so large within the small composition that the cobbler-aggressor seems to be pushing his tailor-victim right out of the picture frame.

Asked by an English interviewer why his Grimm pictures were so small and claustrophobic, Sendak answered, "The tales themselves are claustrophobic. They work on two levels: first, as stories; second, as the unraveling of deep psychological dramas. I'm not so interested in the top layer, the story, as I am in what I think

Opposite: sketch for, and finished art from "Rabbit's Bride," in The Juniper Tree and Other Tales from Grimm. *1973. Sketch: pencil. Finished art: pen-and-ink line. Each 4½ x 3⅝". Left: Victorian brass inkwell*

Above: engraving by Ludwig Grimm for Kinder-und Hausmärchen: Kleine Ausgabe *(1825), from which the artist's composition was derived. Right: from "Hansel and Gretel," in* The Juniper Tree and Other Tales from Grimm. *1973. Pen-and-ink line. 4½ x 3⅝"*

goes on underneath…. I wanted my pictures to tell any readers who think the stories are simple to go back to the beginning and read them again. I didn't want to show Rapunzel with a hank of hair hanging out of a tower. To me that's not what the story is about. A lot of illustrators have chosen that image because there seems little else to draw. But to me, Rapunzel's hair is only the gimmick in the story. I searched for what was really underneath. It was hard. There was not one story that gave up its secret right away." As in "Snow White," the crucial conflict in "Rapunzel" is between age and youth. The witch, Sendak feels, wants desperately to prevent any expression of Rapunzel's sexuality, or any admiration of her beauty.

Questioned further as to whether a young reader has the maturity to understand the meanings implicit in his Grimm illustrations, Sendak said, "I think children read the internal meanings of *everything*. It's only adults who read the top layer most of the time. I'm generalizing again, of course, but I'll bet my pictures don't surprise kids. They know what's in Grimm. They know that stepmother probably means mother, that the word *step* is there to avoid frightening a lot of older people. Children know there are mothers who abandon their children, emotionally if not literally. Sometimes they have to live with this fact. They don't lie to themselves. They wouldn't survive if they did. And my object is never to lie to them."

Left, top and bottom: preliminary sketches for, and right, finished art from "The Fisherman and His Wife," in The Juniper Tree and Other Tales from Grimm. *1973. Preliminary sketches: pencil. Top left: 2 x 2³/₁₆". Bottom left: 5³/₈ x 3³/₄". Finished art: pen-and-ink line. 4¹/₂ x 3⁵/₈"*

To other questioners who ask whether he illustrated for adults or children in *The Juniper Tree*, Sendak responds: "There was a time in history when books like *Alice in Wonderland* and the fairy tales of George MacDonald were read by everybody. They were not designated as being 'for children.' The Grimm tales are about the pure essence of life—incest, murder, insane mothers, love, sex—what have you," Sendak says.

> This is the way life is sometimes, these tales say in the most matter-of-fact way. And this is what I believe children appreciate. People rage against the Grimms' tales, forgetting that originally the brothers had assembled them not for children, but for historical and philological reasons. They were afraid their folk past was being lost in all the political and social upheavals of that period, and the tales were issued as a scholarly edition of peasant stories not to be forgotten as part of the heritage of their homeland. Well, lo and behold, children began to read them. And the second edition was called *The Household Tales* because children were demanding the stories. The point is that those illustrators and writers who attract me are the ones who do not seem to be at all hung up by the fact that their audiences may be small people. They are telling the truth, just the way it is.

The Grimm stories are, of course, rarely about children. As Sendak once remarked, "After all, a twelve-year-old princess is—or was in those days— of marriageable age."

To an interviewer who wondered what relation his work for *The Juniper Tree* bore to his picture books, Sendak observed:

> Grimms' fairy tales are obviously not picture-book material, but they do allow for interpretive illustration. The pictures have as much to say as the text; the trick is to project the same message, but in a different way. It's no good being an illustrator who says a lot that is on his or her mind if that has nothing to do with the text. But to say the same thing that the story is saying in a *personal* way, so as to heighten its meaning, contributes dimension to the tale.
>
> You're not out to do your own *shtick*—you're out merely to do your *shtick* within the confines of the story you're illustrating. Whatever that happens to be—"Hansel and Gretel," "Snow White"—you make it bigger than it was because you have insight into the story as an artist. The illustrator can do a tremendous job of collaboration, of expansion, of illumination. But he

must be discreet. The artist must override the story, but he must also override his own ego for the sake of the story. It is more fun than any other kind of illustration.

For Sendak, illustrating *The Juniper Tree* resulted in a liberating psychological breakthrough. "It was a watershed book for me, one that solved a great many technical and emotional problems," he says. "I found I could now put elements from my own fantasy life together with objective illustration. And, bizarre as the separate pieces might be, I could make them work. I guess I was just old enough and experienced enough to bring it off."

"Illustrating Grimm," he said when it was all over, "was a hard job, which took many years of preparation and concentrated effort. I'm a slow worker, not at all flexible. I couldn't say, 'Oh, Grimm is rough. I think I'll do something else this week.' I could only continue to work on it and nothing else. So I was worn out."

Curiously, for so intense and richly sustained a graphic work, Sendak's illustrations for *The Juniper Tree* have never received any serious criticism as art. There are, today, no publications like the nineteenth-century English magazine *The Studio*, each issue of which was filled with major critical essays on important graphic work.

Certainly there has never been so intense or probing a set of pictures for the Grimms' *Household Tales*. And seldom has so much pictorial content been contained in so compact a space. Yet Sendak, with his unwavering clarity of vision, managed to keep his small pages from ever seeming cluttered, the muchness from ever becoming overmuch. Finally, in the fall of 1973, Farrar, Straus and Giroux published *The Juniper Tree*, one of the few masterly works of book illustration in our time.

Branching Out, Digging Deep

From the spring of 1971 to the spring of 1973, Sendak had concentrated exclusively on his pictures for the Grimm collection, and he was eager to undertake something entirely different for a next project. Yet, when the independent producer Sheldon Riss approached him in 1972 with the proposal to develop and direct an animated film special for television, he hesitated. Those animated TV specials he had watched—and he seldom missed one—never struck him as being special, and the idea of working for a major network filled him with dread. As he explains it, "In the world of book publishing, I have command over my work—how it is printed and presented. I've earned that privilege and I am proud of it. I was afraid of losing it in the world of despotic networks, among the vast crew of collaborators necessary for such an undertaking."

Sendak had, in fact, long wanted to make an animated film. He had even completed two sequences for "Sesame Street" in 1970—one on the number nine entitled *Bumble-Ardy* and another on the number seven entitled *Seven Monsters.* Animation was, as he says, "a deep old love of mine—beginning, as it did for all thirties children, with Walt Disney. The richness of those first Disney shorts, their dazzling impetuosity, guaranteed their claim as a new art form, and the claim survived the test of Disney's first full-length animated features. It's easy now to scorn Disney's famous poor taste, but no creator of animated films since has matched his dramatic gifts. If anything, the anxious emphasis on so-called good

Opposite: preliminary sketch for Outside Over There. *1979. Pencil. 6⅜ x 10".*
Above: preliminary sketch for Outside Over There. *1979. Pencil. 6½ x 6"*

taste today drains the dramatic energy from most contemporary animation—I mean animation done with integrity, not the dread hokum of Saturday-morning TV." The influence of animation and flip-book techniques on Sendak's work is plain, particularly in his earliest books: the endpapers for *A Hole Is to Dig,* the dancing hero in *A Very Special House,* and the entire conception of *What Can You Do with a Shoe?,* among others.

The artist resisted Riss's proposal for more than a year, but, happily, the producer was patient. Once committed to creating an animated film script, Sendak decided to play it safe for his first attempt. He would stick to what he knew best—"those hurdy-gurdy, fantasy-plagued Brooklyn kids." His final scenario incorporated the four books of *The Nutshell Library* within the narrative shell of *The Sign on Rosie's Door.* His admiration for Rosie undiminished by the passage of time, he used his first heroine as the film's leading lady, a kind of Fellini-figure who invents a movie within a movie. Like Sendak's early book on Rosie, the animated film is about the remarkable ability of children to defeat boredom. As Sendak remembers from his own childhood, "Summers were a horror. You couldn't go away, and you couldn't go to school, which at least took up a few hours of the day. For most kids there was really very little to do. The way a child gets through a difficult time is to invent games and make-believe. In *The Sign on Rosie's Door,* Rosie's friends are not nearly as interesting as she is, but she has to make do with them. So she turns them into vassals, and they willingly take bit parts in her fantasies. This is healthy. It gets them through the afternoon. She's lucky to have them, and they're lucky to have her. The kids all use their imagination, that muscle exercised in childhood but not often enough later on."

In Sendak's animated film, *Really Rosie, starring the Nutshell Kids,* the boys of *The Nutshell Library* are Rosie's slaves and, in return, she activates their fantasies. Sendak feels that the marriage of the two works was perfectly logical. "My *Nutshell Library* was always intricately bound to *The Sign on Rosie's Door.* Alligator, Pierre, Johnny, and the nameless hero of *Chicken Soup with Rice* were modeled on the 'men' in Rosie's life; the originals, in fact, appear in *Rosie's Door* under their real names."

The young rock composer Carole King set Sendak's scenario to music. He was delighted with the results. "She added her own emotional quality and gave my words a reverberation that they didn't originally have," Sendak says. "They've taken on a new edge and weight." Sendak's characters, of course, had changed somewhat, too, in the years intervening between books and film: the artist's style had altered so that the children he invented for the screen, while based on those in *The Nutshell Library* and *Rosie's Door,* looked different, were amplified versions of the originals.

In the five quick story-board sketches, dated July 1973, that Sendak provided to guide the animator of the sequences containing Rosie and Buttermilk, her cat, it's readily apparent how much more accomplished the artist has become since 1960. Rosie's too-big costume now hangs with a good deal more authority. With her black boa and long black gloves, she resembles a mini-version of Toulouse-Lautrec's Yvette Guilbert. (It was from story-boards, rendered by the artist, that the several animators working on *Really Rosie* prepared the hundreds of variations of pose, gesture, and expression required to bring Sendak's illustrated characters to life on the screen. The artist himself did hundreds of guide-drawings of Rosie and her gang for the film's animation crew. Again, though the various animators followed Sendak's style, each brought his or her own personality to bear on the work. (Each *Nutshell* story had a different animator, as did Rosie. Sendak felt that the animator of *Alligators All Around* was particularly successful in breathing new life into this nonsense alphabet.)

The artist also painted a number of tenderly evocative background scenes for the film: a view of Brooklyn rooftops with laundry wafting in the breeze (see page 21); a nostalgic rendering of the street where Rosie lived (actually it was a street some blocks away from the real Rosie's house, which he found to be "a nightmare of brand-new siding" when he revisited it); a rendition of the famous cellar door, behind which Rosie and her entourage retreated when the rain began.

As for fresh material needed to enable the film to run its allotted twenty-four minutes of the half-hour-special time, Sendak looked back through some two dozen sketchbooks of Rosie dialogue, drawings, and ideas that he had collected during 1948 and 1949. One Rosie incident he added resulted in the film's song "Did You Hear What Happened to Chicken Soup?," all about a character of that name who supposedly dies after choking on a chicken bone. "Now that came from a real incident," Sendak explains. "I watched Rosie do the scene. She was the kind of a kid who could control her friends only if she could grab them imaginatively; otherwise they could be very cruel to her. If she didn't have a movie to tell or an act to do, they abandoned her instantly, as children will. Or they made fun of her. But once she got hold of something to dramatize, she had them.

> I remember one day—I wrote it all down—they were sitting on the stoop and talking busily—everybody except Rosie, who sat by herself on the top step. She was trying to get their attention, and she said that magic sentence, "Did you hear who died?" I mean that's going to get anybody, including me. I looked up. They looked up and said, "Who?" And she said, "My grand-mother, early this morning."

I knew her grandmother. I had seen her out the window, brushing the carpets and yelling in Italian at Rosie in the street. And I believed Rosie—we all did. Then she went into a pantomime of what had happened in the early dawn hours when they heard furniture collapsing and mirrors breaking and this rather heavy woman gagging and choking, and rushing about. They hung her head out the window. They gave her the Kiss of Life. All to no avail. "Where is the body?" the kids asked. "Gone. Cops came fast—all over." And Rosie told it with a kind of tremulous voice. I mean she was the Eleanora Duse of Bensonhurst.

Now during this telling of the story, up the street comes the grandmother, two big shopping bags in hand, her carpet slippers flapping, and she goes up the steps cursing the kids violently in Italian, brushing them aside with her feet, waddling into the house. They all separated for her, then said, "Tell us again, Rosie."

For a year, Sendak served as scriptwriter, lyricist, director, and apprentice animator of his film, an experience he found exhilarating—the fulfillment of a child movie-lover's dream. He also made two trips to Los Angeles to work with Miss King on the songs. "It turned out to be a real Brooklyn project," he says with pleasure. "Both Sheldon Riss and Carole King grew up in the same neighborhoods as I did." Finally, the film was fully edited, polished, and ready for viewing. *Really Rosie, starring the Nutshell Kids* was originally televised over CBS in February 1975, and was repeated the following June.

Those who saw the artist's first effort on film praised its honesty and the refreshing sense of real children with real children's concerns that it projected. *Rosie* had a wit, humor, and panache rarely found in an animated film for young children. When CBS decided not to run the film again, Weston Woods, a firm specializing in film strips of children's books for the institutional market, acquired the rights to it, and *Rosie* is now a holiday special in schools and libraries throughout the country. As a memento, Sendak has hanging in his house in Ridgefield a color photograph of an authentic theatrical billboard on Broadway announcing Rosie's TV-film premiere.

Early in 1975, Sendak had begun to do new sketches for the story-board of what was to have been his second film, an animated version of *Very Far Away*. These drawings, too, were far more accomplished and appealing than those done for the book in 1957. But the artist abandoned the project when he became disenchanted with network television.

In the spring of 1976, however, Sendak illustrated a book that would never

Story-board sketches for
animated film of Very Far
Away. 1975. Pen-and-ink
line and watercolor.
From a sheet of sketches,
10½ x 13½"

have had the sort of illustrations it did were it not for his experience with animation. *Some Swell Pup, or Are You Sure You Want a Dog?*, which he characterizes as "a dog *pre*-training manual for children," is done in broad, brilliantly colored, funny-papers style, an approach directly related to the two years he had just spent doing story-board drawings for *Rosie*. The book was written by Sendak and a professional dog trainer, Matthew Margolis. Unfortunately, several critics chose to compare the work to Sendak's most recent book, *The Juniper Tree*, rather than consider it on its own merits. They saw the dog manual as trivial and repetitive.

Any repetitions, however, had been purely intentional. "One of the pleasures of the comic strip," Sendak says, "is that you can be so graphic and direct that the learning process is less painful for the reader. You can totally obliterate the quality of teaching-ness. Because children are so easily bored, the lessons of *Some Swell Pup* are all hidden within the pictures, and that's why they can and should be repeated for effect. On the surface it's a comic book."

In *Some Swell Pup*, Sendak's Io is cast in the role of an irresistible infant canine who is acquired by Sendak's familiar boy and girl characters. (The pair had last starred in "King Grisly-Beard," a lighthearted version of a Grimm fairy tale done for *Family Circle* magazine in 1973 and published the same year by Farrar, Straus and Giroux. The artist refers to his heroine as "an aggressive and hysterical *yenta* [a complainer and nag]" and his hero as "a passive and selfish kid."

It doesn't take the two children long to discover that puppies urinate, defecate, scratch, and chew at will. They are, of course, horrified by such uncivilized, "disgusting" behavior, until they are made to see the light. A wise old character, played by a grown dog, explains that these traits are as much a part of any puppy's nature as being cute. If they want to own a dog, then they must behave consistently. They should not yell or pick up their animal by the scruff of the neck. Above all, they must be gentle. "A pre-training manual," says Sendak, "shows how to establish a relationship between yourself and the animal. . . . This is the socialization of the child and the animal: coming to accept the puppy's nature, understanding that its musculature is not controllable. You cannot actually begin training a dog until he is at least ten to twelve weeks old, but you can do a lot to make him untrainable before that time."

Of his collaborator on *Some Swell Pup*, Sendak says, "Matthew helped me to see my own intractable dogs without anger—with patience." Sendak had already trained Io and Erda by himself, or so he thought. But, accustomed to a small dog like Jennie, he was totally unprepared for walking a full-grown golden retriever and German shepherd. "I was as bad as the kids in the book," Sendak remembers. "The dogs would drag me down the road. I'd get mad and scream and yell. Here I was, a man who'd had a coronary, and I was supposed to walk. Sure. But I was racing after them! I think they still wonder when I'm going to go bananas again. . . . Before Matthew and I could even retrain them, a new rapport had to be established. I was ferociously disappointed in them, in part because I still missed Jennie, but also because they weren't as smart or as quick as she was. They had become my whipping boys. I had to learn how to appreciate their natures; animals are capable of only so much. We need to understand the limits of their abilities."

Margolis helped to clear the air. And, as Sendak came to accept his own dogs for what they were individually, they each became interesting to him. When Sendak decided to keep Erda's only surviving son, Agamemnon, he immediately called in Margolis to help him start out right. "And then I had an exciting insight," the artist recalls. "You can manage puppies—or babies, for that matter—if you don't project your old enemy-figures on them." This is what *Some Swell Pup* is about.

Yet this modest—and to the artist "vitally important"—book brought him the worst notices of his career. What seemed to outrage the largest number of people was the fact that the puppy relieves himself on the floor, not once but several times. "Sendak is up front about dog droppings," began one negative review. The artist was upset by the book's poor reception. "Adults are so hung up on toilet training that they can't see straight. It doesn't bother the kids. They know that puppies go to the bathroom on the floor." As for those who complained about the book's tedium or lack of getting anywhere, this was, in fact, both the nature of

Sendak's subject matter and the burden of the book's message. Much of the early weeks spent with puppies seems to go nowhere. Dog ownership and training—or child rearing, for that matter—are vocations that people are drawn into all too easily because of their surface pleasures and charm. Babies and puppies alike are irresistibly cute, but their proper upbringing is more than fifty percent tedium— a fact that most children and adults are unaware of at the outset. By frequent graphic repetition of the puppy's most maddening natural traits, Sendak, without ever preaching, drives this important lesson home. And, as he points out, "Of course, the book is not really about dogs at all; any child sees through that immediately. The dog in the book serves just as easily as a metaphor for children."

If the levity of *Some Swell Pup*'s art disappointed some of Sendak's fans, there could be no doubt of the seriousness and virtuosity of Sendak's black-and-white illustrations for Randall Jarrell's last book for children, *Fly by Night*, published in the fall of 1976. These had been a long time in coming, because the artist so missed the close collaborative relationship he had had with the poet on their two previous books together. Were it not for the courage he had gained from his work on *The Juniper Tree*, Sendak doubts that he would have been able to come to terms with Jarrell's last children's book. "My satisfaction with the Grimm, with weaving bits of my own fantasy life into the various tales, gave me a self-confidence I'd never before had." The artist was also able to use many of the drawings of meadows and sheep sketched in Wales, during the summer of 1972, in the Jarrell book.

"*Fly by Night* is a strange story," Sendak says, "and a very personal one." It is a fantasy about a young boy who can fly—or at least float through the air—when he goes to sleep at night. The story concerns one of the hero's dream adventures, during which he encounters a family of owls. "It is a painful dream," the artist feels, "about a little boy who misses his mother's presence, and I knew this was something that had always troubled Randall. So I substituted my mother for his mother, and I used the occasion to express feelings about my mother in graphic terms. She appears all through the book—as a shepherdess, as an immigrant girl coming to America, and as a young mother holding her babies. I put her there for him, and that made it our collaboration."

In all instances, the pictures of Sendak's mother came from family snapshots. The jacket illustration, in which she wears a large brimmed hat (her wedding hat) and carries—somewhat incongruously—a shepherd's crook, comes from a photograph taken soon after her marriage to Philip Sendak. The double-page illustration of the flying boy, nude, shows him soaring over Sendak as a baby in his mother's arms. Using the snapshot of the three Sendak children with their mother, the artist here turns his two siblings into lambs. "I had an older brother, the sensitive one, and a sister, the brainy one, of whom I was jealous," Sendak explains. "I was the spoiled one." So he took this belated opportunity to remove them both from the competition for maternal affection by transforming them into defense-less lambs. "I'm that wolf too, walking nearby," he says, "probably thinking about devouring lambs." His mother appears a second time in the same illustration, looking young and vulnerable (as she surely was when she first came to the United States from Poland) and playing the role of shepherdess. Above the entire scene, a commandingly large owl's head looms, eyes aglow. It dominates the illustration much as the mother owl and her bedtime story dominate the boy's dream.

The drawings are meticulously rendered, with a sharp pen line and much landscape detail. "What I'd like to think the art is like," Sendak says, "is not an illustrator's work at all, but a writer's—Kafka's. He could describe a dream scene in quick, matter-of-fact strokes. The description is absolutely prosaic, entirely literal, but the effect is surreal. Dreams are never far out graphically. They are intensely real, which is what gives them their hallucinatory quality."

This quality is amply present in the artwork for *Fly by Night,* and is due, in part, to the at first jarring incongruity of Sendak's mother and Sendak as a baby appearing in the dream of a child who is so obviously an Anglo-Saxon. David, the seven-year-old hero whom we first see perched on a tree limb, his chow dog stand-ing below, is an all-American type—he'd be perfectly at home in a Grant Wood painting. Thus, there is something odd about finding the artist's East European Jewish mother playing so central a part in David's dream. Other touches contrib-ute to the hallucinatory effect. Two rabbits appear, far larger than they ever would be in real life. The boy-dreamer's eyes are closed throughout the book—a discon-certing element until the reader remembers that a dreamer sees with his mind's eye.

There were, as always, those critics who protested against the hero's nudity, a criticism the artist had tried his best to avoid. "I drew the boy first with pajamas on, but he looked too much like Wee Willie Winkie. Then I tried him in under-wear, and the picture looked like an ad for Fruit of the Loom. I even tried him wrapped in sheets and blankets, but it was too baroque. He had to be naked. But I knew they'd say it was just like me, arbitrarily making somebody nude." John Updike, in a *New York Times Book Review* discussion of the work and its psychosex-ual aspects, in fact, made a passing reference to David's "inviting derrière," a comment which angered the artist as being totally beside the point.

While *Fly by Night* represented Sendak at his most serious and self-involved, *Seven Little Monsters,* also published in 1976, revealed the artist as confectioner—a dispenser of cotton-candy-weight graphics. Actually, the book was one that had

Opposite: from Fly by Night. *1976. Pen-and-ink line. 5⁵⁄₁₆ x 8¼"*

been put together and published in Europe a year earlier by Sendak's German-language publisher, Daniel Keel. It came from drawings done some years earlier for one of the "Sesame Street" number sequences. The seven little monsters of the title—two of whom are first cousins to Wild Things—terrorize the still littler inhabitants of a small Old World town. Each has his own specialty: one jumps high, another can unscrew his head, a third can drill holes with his nose, and so on. The book makes no pretense to being an important Sendak work; it has only sixteen pages, plus a charming nursery-frieze fold-out of all the story's pictures. But *Seven Little Monsters* also has a disconcerting flaw. The sixth monster, hairy, dark, and horned in the opening group picture of the monsters assembled, appears later in the story as blond, unhorned, and dressed in a belted coat. There is no way that these two monsters could be one and the same. Though the artist had nothing to do with the transformation of pictures for a proposed film strip into those for a slight book, he would surely have rectified the inconsistency had it been brought to his attention. As it was, the finished work made him look careless. Again the book was not enthusiastically received. Sendak's audience had come to expect more.

When *Some Swell Pup* failed to make the preliminary list for the Caldecott Medal in 1976, and when the children's-book review media that had always treated him with respect, if not perfect understanding, now gave vent to strong negative feelings about one or more of his recent books, Sendak said with some bewilderment, "I've had the most savage reviews of my career; it must be a 'Get Sendak' year."

At the end of that same year, as if in unconscious response to his critics, Sendak returned to the genre he knew and loved best: the picture book. It was in no way a willed return, because, as he has made clear on several occasions, he does not choose—or plot—his books in any rational way. Rather, certain inexplicable feelings well up inside him and, unbidden, force their way out. The start is almost like automatic writing. "I have the first lines of my new picture book!" he told a caller excitedly in December 1976. "It's so dense already that I can't get beyond them. I'm not even sure I know what they mean.

"But I'll get there," he said confidently. "My unconscious knows exactly what they are, only I don't know with my thinking mind, but every day I get a little clue. 'Listen, dumdum, here's a word for you. See what you can make of it.' So my unconscious throws it out and I catch it: 'Oh, a word, fantastic!' And then I do without for three days, and the unconscious says, 'This man's too much to believe; he walks, he thinks, he sits, he doesn't do anything, he's a bore, throw him another word, otherwise he'll sit there forever and have a coronary.'"

Opposite: from Some Swell Pup. *1976. Pen-and-ink line, with watercolor separations. 7¹³/₁₆ x 6¼"*

218

CHICKEN SOUP WITH RICE ~ May 2.74

MODEL: BUSBY BERKELEY   EMBLEM: SOUP BOWL   MOOD: EXTRAVAGANT   COLORS: NIGHT KITCHEN   DANCES: TAP-SHAG-ROCKETT LINEUP

(LOOK AT DANCES IN 'FOOTLIGHT PARADE / 42nd ST. / GOLDDIGGERS OF '33 f'35) TAKE OFF IN THE MANNER OF DANCE OF THE HOURS - FANTASIA - PARODY.

Books to Study décor: B. Berkeley Book
Gotta Sing Gotta Dance

Tuesday: Close up of kids appearing in Chorus line-up from left. - all white backgrand - pull away - white is Bowl of Soup - they are skating on edge of Saucer - New York Skyline - Chicken Soup can buildings - an Sipping Chorus - Rosie appears out of Bowl with giant Spoons. they should all be in winter costume.

First flap: preliminary drawings for animated film of Really Rosie, *starring the Nutshell Kids. 1974. Pencil and watercolor. Each 9 x 12". Gatefold: background painting from animated film of* Really Rosie, *starring the Nutshell Kids. 1974. Pencil and watercolor. 10¼ x 78". Above: artist's notes and rough sketches for "Chicken Soup with Rice" production number in animated film* Really Rosie, *starring the Nutshell Kids. 1974. Pencil and watercolor. 9 x 12"*

The first five lines Sendak spoke of were these:

> When Papa was away at Sea
> And Mama in the Arbor,
> Ida played her Wonder Horn
> to rock the Baby still,
> but never watched!

"Is it the right time for a book?" Sendak mused. "It's like getting pregnant when you've just gone crazy and you've found out your house has burned down. I'm definitely with life, as they say, sitting like a mother on a stump, thinking: 'Thank you, God, thank you.'"

Outside Over There (1981), the third and last work in Sendak's self-styled picture-book trilogy, would appear eleven years after the second, *In the Night Kitchen*, and eighteen years after the first, *Where the Wild Things Are*. He views the three works as a unit because "They are all variations on the same theme: how children master various feelings—anger, boredom, fear, frustration, jealousy—and manage to come to grips with the realities of their lives." Each book has a place-name for a title, a fantasy locale where the major action of the story takes place. The curious genesis of *Outside Over There* as the most recent book's title is revealed in a piece Sendak himself wrote in February 1975, on the occasion of *Really Rosie*'s CBS premiere. "I loved Rosie. She knew how to get through a day . . . Rosie [is] the living thread, the connecting link, between me in my window and the outside over there. I did, finally, get outside over there. In 1956, after illustrating some twenty books by various writers, I did a Rosie and wrote my own." In some way deeply meaningful to the artist, *Outside Over There* represents his ultimate "doing a Rosie."

When Sendak had just begun working on *Outside Over There*, he confided to the interviewer Jonathan Cott, "This last part of my trilogy is going to be the strangest. *Wild Things* now seems to me to be a very simple book—its simplicity is probably what made it successful, but I could never be that simple again. *Night Kitchen* I much prefer—it reverberates on double levels. But this third book will reverberate on triple levels." More than a year later, while still working on the book, Sendak told an audience of writers, teachers, and aficionados of children's literature that the development of *Outside Over There* was "chaotic." "My stories come in bits and pieces of memories that don't seem related for a very long time," said the artist. "But something in me determines they will be related; they're going to work together, come hell or high water. It's a kind of predetermined thing."

What are some of these bits and pieces? As with other Sendak works, *Outside*

Over There grew organically, in part at least, from work that had preceded it. The frontispiece to *The Juniper Tree* was a drawing for a little-known Grimm tale called "The Goblins," about the stealing of a baby. The tale's aura of mystery so captured the artist's imagination that he used it as the bare-bones plot of his new book. The heroine of the book, Ida, developed from the artist's conception of Gretel in the Grimm collection—that first conventionally beautiful heroine he had drawn. Another important influence in the work was a book Sendak had seen as a child:

> I must have been five or six years old, and in the next apartment lived a girl my age who had marvelous books, like the Big Little Book of *David Copperfield*, with photographs of Freddie Bartholomew in it. That's who I thought David Copperfield was for a very long time. She also had another book that we read continuously on the landing outside our apartments. It was a ritual book with us, and it had to do with a little girl who takes a walk and is caught in a storm. At the beginning, she is wearing her mother's raincoat, which is far too big for her, and she's carrying an umbrella. There is a juxtaposition of her walking in this flowing garment in clear weather and then, suddenly, in the very next picture—which seemed to me miraculous, like a transformation—the sky is dark; the wind is blowing against her; she is billowing out like a great yellow cloud, her umbrella inside out.

The artist has no recollection of the book's title or ending, but the storm picture has stayed with him over the years. "And with it," Sendak says,

> the need, for some creative reason, to get that little girl into a book. It is now more than forty years that I've been pushing her into a book. I was a little disappointed as I grew older, because I got to know the Morton Salt container, and I thought everybody knew who she was. But I don't think that's the right girl. Later on, there was the Uneeda Biscuit boy, who looked very solemn in a long yellow rain-slicker, but that was a *he*, not a *she*, so I've never found out who this child was.
>
> The next thing that happened was that I realized I had now been living in rural Connecticut for six years, and the setting of my book would have to change. All my other locales have been urban—New York children, I suppose. It took a long time for me to adjust to living in the country, but I'm getting there slowly. So I wanted my heroine to be a country child. Now

I had to work with a little girl trapped in the rain in the country, and she would have something to do with goblins who steal a baby. It all settled in very well with me.

Somehow, when Sendak put all these elements together, the "country" was transformed from the artist's modern Ridgefield to Grimm country in the eighteenth century. Perhaps making use of "The Goblins" illustration from Grimm seemed to require a fairy-tale setting removed in time. While he worked on the illlustrations for *Outside Over There*, Sendak listened exclusively to the music of Mozart. As he explains, "I wanted only the sound of Mozart for this book. And I made my own make-believe connections: 'This is Grimm country; this is the eighteenth century; Mozart died in 1791; it's proper the music should be only Mozart.' Since I am running the show, I can do things any way I like."

Sendak even borrowed certain images from Mozart. "One of the dénouements in *Outside Over There*," he confesses, "is stolen directly from *The Magic Flute*. And I have done an *hommage* to Mozart as well—at the very end of the book, when the crisis is over and all is reasonably well—only reasonably well—and Ida is going home tired. She wanders through a wood. In the distance is a little cottage, and a silhouetted figure sits inside, busily writing and composing. It's Mozart working on *The Magic Flute*. [The artist used the same image on a Mahler record-album cover he was commissioned to do during this same period.] These are the games that you play; after long hours by yourself you've got to do something to entertain yourself."

The artist feels that his illustrations for *Outside Over There* owe a decided debt to the two Sendak works immediately preceding it: *Some Swell Pup* and *Fly by Night*. Certainly the clear, bright palette of the first influenced the brilliant colors of the painterly illustrations in *Outside Over There*. And Ida, the heroine, could never have floated so gracefully through the air without Sendak's having worked out several technical difficulties on the airborne hero of the Jarrell work.

But, to begin with, there were the words. Not many of the artist's admirers are aware of how seriously he takes the texts of his own tales. *Outside Over There*, a story with only 359 words, took almost a year and a half—and more than one hundred drafts—to complete. "I have a hostility toward books which are not well written," Sendak says. "Because the picture book is such a beautiful, poetic form, I feel it should be treated with the utmost respect." Though he invariably draws to music in his sunlit studio, he writes in a perfectly silent room, orange rubber plugs stuffed into his ears. "Writing is the most private business," he says, "and much more difficult than illustrating. I know that I would not be an illustrator without

Overleaf: preliminary drawing for Outside Over There. *1979. Pencil. 6⅜ x 20"*

229

words. I've never done a book that was any good unless the text excited me. And my own texts have to be very good, as far as I'm concerned, before I illustrate them."

When Sendak was, at last, satisfied with the text of *Outside Over There,* he sent it to his editor, Ursula Nordstrom. "I was ready to bear her onslaughts," he says, "and, of course, onslaughts there were." Mostly, these took the form of questions about Ida's actions and motivations—and how much the words, rather than the pictures, should convey. Once author and editor were content with a working text, Sendak began immediately to make a small-size dummy, about 3½ by 2½ inches.

For the study drawings he did for *Outside Over There,* Sendak, for the first time in his career, supervised the taking of a series of photographs by a professional photographer friend. The artist had previously chosen two children to play the roles of Ida and her baby sister from a group of color Polaroids of possible candidates. The older girl, about nine, who was to be Ida, was a wonderfully soulful, Spanish-looking child named Esme. The baby, Natalie, was about fourteen months old "and built like a brick wall," according to the artist. "I mean solid."

Sendak posed the children very much as he wanted his final drawings to look. Esme was dressed in an old-fashioned nightgown for the occasion (which the artist adapted for the costume Ida would wear in the final artwork), and she carried baby Natalie like a sack of laundry. "It was really the only way I could ever get the proper feel for the bulk of a fourteen-month-old baby as picked up by a nine-year-old child," Sendak explains. "These are realistic touches that just can't be fudged, and I wanted to get them absolutely right." Sendak also brought along a favorite prop for Natalie to wear: that same droll bonnet resembling a lampshade which had been worn by the Bee-Man of Orn as a baby. The artist was delighted with the results of his first formal photographic sittings. "The pictures have a super-real stopped-in-time quality," he reported. "They're better than I had any right to hope for." He compares this set of photographs to "architectural drawings preliminary to beginning work on a project." His finished illustrations retain the near-hallucinatory quality of the photographs, but, stylistically, are more painterly, fluid, and accomplished than any previous Sendak color work. He confesses to having borrowed freely from a turn-of-the-century German painter, Phillip Otto Runge, most particularly from a painting of his titled *The Hülsenbeck Children.* The artist admired the intentional distortion and staring eyes of Runge's subjects.

Ida, the heroine of *Outside Over There,* is pluckier than any Sendak hero or heroine to date. The author/artist, in fact, is full of admiration for Ida's courage and ability to take action despite her own fears and her jealousy of her lost sibling. Sendak agonized a good deal, however, over his heroine's name. Was it the right one? It contained Id—all to the good, because Ida was a primal child. The name

Opposite: preliminary drawing for Outside Over There. *1979. Pencil. 9 x 10"*

was also auspicious in that it belonged to Mrs. Ida Perles, the Sendak children's second mother as they were growing up in Brooklyn. But something about the name still nagged at him. Only after the book had been delivered to Harper and Row did Sendak realize that the letters of Ida also appear, backwards, in his mother's name—Sadie. The artist was delighted. Moreover, he is certain that he had already subconsciously known this fact when he wrote the lines:

> If Ida backwards in the rain
> Would only turn around again

Though Ida is unquestionably the heroine, in some way Sendak considers that the story is really the baby's. It is to her that something terrible happens. And Sendak's feelings are as much engaged on her behalf as on the heroine's. While working on the pictures, he said to a friend, "You know, my sister Natalie was

234

exactly Ida's age when she took care of me as a baby. And the last time we saw each other, I asked whether anything had ever happened to me while she was taking care of me." Natalie could remember nothing of significance. Sendak was not expecting to hear that he'd been taken by goblins, but he so felt the story in which he was immersed that he would not have been surprised to hear Natalie say "yes" and relate some incident that would account for his empathy with Ida's baby sister.

The goblins in *Outside Over There* number five, and it has occurred to the artist that this undoubtedly had something to do with the Dionne quintuplets. "No one who was a child in the thirties could fail to think in terms of those five babies. We saw pictures of them every time they smiled, cut a tooth, or got a new toy."

The two big, continuing stories of the thirties were, in fact, the kidnapping of the Lindbergh baby and the birth and rearing of the Dionne quintuplets. The first was a horror story that couldn't fail to frighten a small child; the second was a kind of contemporary fairy tale: five children taken from their natural parents and brought up like fairy princesses.

Ursula Nordstrom recalls a time during the sixties when a plane had been sent to Brazil to rescue some missionaries stranded in a remote jungle outpost where several whites had already been killed by a primitive tribe. "Maurice was in the office that day, and we spoke of it. He remarked that the rescue plane was a Fairchild and its name— 'fair child'—made him think of the Lindbergh baby for the first time in years." That the Lindbergh child was somewhere in the back of Sendak's mind when he was drawn to the Grimms' tale of the goblins' kidnapping seems certain. In *Outside Over There*, Sendak's goblins use a ladder to reach their victim, and then leave it behind—just as the Lindbergh kidnapper did.

The final work in his picture-book trilogy was finished early in June 1979, but Sendak found it difficult to turn it in to his publisher. It was tantamount to permitting a cherished private vision to go public. For weeks before he took the artwork into New York from Ridgefield, he dreamed variations of the same dream: of having a baby which is taken away from him. Finally, right after his fifty-first birthday, he hired a limousine for the occasion and accompanied the original illustrations to Harper. The entire children's book staff, as well as representatives from the publishing firm's top management, were on hand to welcome the artist, and a bottle of Piper-Heidsieck was opened for the occasion. Most gratifying to the artist, however, was learning that for the first time in his career, a Sendak picture book was scheduled to be sold and promoted in both the children's and adult's book markets. "I had waited a long time to be taken out of kiddy-book land and allowed to join the artists of America," Sendak says.

Mozart: Quartet No. 19 in C, K. 465 ("Dissonant")

Recurring Themes

Anyone familiar with Sendak's work knows that certain images and themes recur from book to book, year after year. The subject of food and eating—or being eaten up, for one, has been a central concern since the artist was a child. Recalling the intense pleasure he experienced on receiving his first real book, *The Prince and the Pauper,* as a ninth-birthday gift from his sister, Natalie, he reported, "I remember trying to bite it." This was his ultimate sensual reaction; he had first noticed how beautiful it was, how good it smelled, and how solid and smooth it was to the touch. The description is reminiscent of a younger child's perception of that first love object: the mother. Sendak's earliest impressions of New York City, too, are intimately related to food and eating. To want to taste something—to eat—is an expression of pure pleasure, and love.

Yet eating can be something else as well. In *Kenny's Window,* the first story Sendak wrote as well as illustrated, the hero, Kenny, laughingly suggests "Let's eat Bucky!" when the toys he has invited to an impromptu party ask, "What shall we eat?" Bucky is a beloved teddy bear, but also a tyrant of sorts, who often makes Kenny angry. The threat to eat someone up is a thinly disguised cover for fierce feelings of anger and aggression. In the *Nutshell Library* quartet, the misanthropic hero of *One Was Johnny* warns his nine unwanted guests: "I'll start to count backwards and when I am through—if this house isn't empty I'll eat all of you!!!!" and in *Pierre,* the lion—himself a metaphoric projection of the hero's own aggression—carries out this very threat by making a meal of the indifferent Pierre.

Food—or the lack of it—is a crucial element in *Where the Wild Things Are.* For talking back to his mother (angrily threatening to eat her up), Max is sent to bed "without eating anything," and this is more than half the reason for his rage. Once he has made himself king of all wild things and has presided over a triumphal wild rumpus, however, Max willingly gives up his throne when "all around from far away across the world he smelled good things to eat." And the book's perfect ending is achieved as Max, back in his very own room, finds "his supper waiting for him, and it was still hot." The small listener instinctively knows that where there is hot food, there is also forgiveness and maternal love restored.

In Sendak's next picture book, *Hector Protector and As I Went over the Water,* both nursery-rhyme improvisations revolve around food and eating. Hector, the ill-tempered messenger, deliberately sets off without his edible dispatch—the cake his mother is sending to the Queen. The entire pictorial interpretation is a comic consideration of unloving behavior (the withholding of food by the hero) and its punishment (food being withheld from the hero). The companion rhyme, *As I Went over the Water,* begins with an act of oral aggression: a disconcertingly cheerful, underwater monster swallows a ship whole. With the behemoth's regurgitation of the ship, all feelings of aggression are presumably assuaged, and the entire cast—small sea captain, sea predator, and two toothless blackbirds—are last viewed as a comradely foursome.

In Sendak's *Higglety Pigglety Pop!,* eating is the dog-heroine Jennie's consuming passion. Voraciously, she devours all the sandwiches a pig has to offer, wolfs down a milk-wagon-full of dairy products, and then gets an unsuspecting parlormaid to whip her up a batch of buttermilk pancakes because she is, presumably, faint from hunger. An unfulfilled artist, Jennie cannot find food enough (or love enough?) in this world to satisfy her. Perhaps this is the meaning of her existential lament, "There must be more to life than having everything." Only when she wins the leading lady's role in the World Mother Goose Theatre is she able to satisfy her insatiable appetite. (Jennie's part requires her to consume a mop made out of salami during every performance.) An artist's ultimate satisfaction is in the practice of her—or his—art; it is food for the spirit and the means of achieving immortality.

In the Night Kitchen is, from beginning to end, a paean to the sights, sounds, and smells of that most familiar and comforting childhood haven, the kitchen. If warmth and love dominate its food-filled province, there is also an element of danger. Mickey, the hero, is almost consumed—baked in a cake for others to eat.

Ultimately, however, Mickey the pilot helps to feed us all, by providing "cake every morning," thus fulfilling the artist's childhood longing to be able to watch, and perhaps to join, the Sunshine Bakers at their nighttime labors. As it did in *Wild Things,* food provides the perfect grace note on which to end a joyous dream about the sensual pleasures of being a young child.

When the question of food is raised, Sendak says, "The business of eating is such an immensely important part of life for a child. The Grimms' tales are full of things being eaten and then disgorged. It's an image that constantly appeals to me, and to most children, too. The scene where the monster eats the boat and regurgitates it in *As I Went over the Water* struck me as hilarious when I drew it. I have the mind of a child.

Of a fantasy sketch in which a child is depicted devouring its mother, he admits, "On the face of it, what could be more destructive? But, in fact, the child may not view it in that light. It's the most natural thing. There's that great, luminous breast hanging over your head; if you have that much of the mother, why not more? Obviously she's there for you. There's something both monstrous and poignant about it."

Sendak is himself interested in eating, often those foods that were treats during his childhood. Though he eats spartanly during the workweek—in the summer and fall mostly vegetables from his own garden—whenever a visitor comes to his house in Ridgefield, the artist requests "a corned-beef sandwich, please, and something marvelously rich and chocolate and gooey for dessert."

Since food ranks high in Sendak's lexicon of pleasures, it is no surprise that he worries excessively about his dogs' appetites. When his German shepherd Agamemnon was still a puppy, something of a power struggle developed between him and his master. "Aggy sensed my anxiety about food and would refuse to eat," Sendak recalls. "It became a battle of wills, and he usually won." To this day, Sendak insists on perfect quiet in the house when the three dogs come in at 5:00 P.M. to have their dinner. He is not above sending visitors upstairs, or outdoors, to enforce the rule.

If anything looms larger than food in Sendak's work, particularly in his later work, it is babies. From the comically irresistible cartoon in *The Bee-Man of Orn* of the Bee-Man transformed back into babyhood, to the first use of family photographs to depict infants in *Zlateh the Goat,* the artist has exhibited a marked affinity for babies as subjects. In *Higglety Pigglety Pop!,* Sendak, for the first time, used a photograph of himself to fashion the character of Baby. In 1968, the artist drew an arresting frontal view of a nude baby girl floating in air—MacDonald's *Light Princess* as an infant. For *The Juniper Tree* in 1973, Sendak provided the command-

Following pages: fantasy sequences. Pen-and-ink line. Page 240: 1952. 10 x 7⅝". Page 241: 1957. 5⅜ x 7⅜". Page 242: drawn to Deems Taylor's Through the Looking Glass. *1957. 10 x 7⅝". Page 243: drawn to Brahms'* Violin Concerto. *1955. 10 x 7½". Page 244: 1966. 11 x 8⅜". 8⅜". Page 245: drawn to Beethoven's* Quartet in F, Opus 135. *1975. 10 x 7⅝". Page 246: drawn to Schubert's* Die Winterreise. *1977. 11 x 8½".*

Through The Looking Glass
Deems Taylor – Feb 25, '57

Jan. 2, '55
Brahms Violin Concerto

Beethoven - Quartet in F, Op. 135 - "IT MUST BE"

M Sendak
Nov. 23, 75

DIE
WINTER REISE
FEB. 26, 77

ing frontispiece baby for "The Goblins." In Randall Jarrell's *Fly by Night*, the artist again made use of himself as a baby, this time enfolded in his mother's arms. During the seventies, too, Sendak did two drawings of babies for the Op-Ed page of the *New York Times*, one of a somewhat dubious-looking infant proffering a toast to the new year, another of an infant in thrall before a television set. And in *Outside Over There*, not only did Sendak use posed photographs of an infant in order to develop one of his two leading characters, he turned to a German photographic album to characterize the five goblin babies, the villains of the tale.

On an obvious level, the artist's interest in babies can be attributed to his fascination with his own childhood and babyhood. In each of the works of his picture-book trilogy, there is a progressively younger hero or heroine. Max of *Wild Things* is older than Mickey of *Night Kitchen*, who, in turn, is older than the baby in *Outside Over There*.

The decade of the thirties was, in many ways, baby-obsessed. Beyond the continuing news stories on the Dionne quintuplets and the latest developments in the Lindbergh kidnapping case, babies, in general, were exploited. The comedian Eddie Cantor starred in a film seen by Sendak, *Kid Millions*, in which the workers in a milk factory are dressed like infants. There was also the comedienne Fannie Brice, who appeared in movies and was heard weekly over the radio in the role of Baby Snooks. And it was the decade of child movie stars. Sendak remembers "the cheated, missed-luck look in my father's eyes as he turned from the radiant image of Shirley Temple back to the three un-golden children he'd begotten. Ah, the wonderful, rich, American-dream blessing of having a Shirley Temple girl and a Bobby Breen boy! I never forgave those yodeling, tap-dancing, brimming-with-glittering-life miniature monsters."

From the time Sendak first read Dorothy Baruch's case study of a disturbed child, *One Little Boy*, and was moved by her documentation that "the thoughts of childhood are deep and dark," he has been looking back at his own childhood and trying to unravel "this loose mystery of myself, the psychic reality of my own childhood." At the time he was working on *Outside Over There*, Sendak was fascinated by a study of preverbal language, the signals babies give to make their needs and wants known. And as an artist, he has long been intrigued by "the physicalness of babies, the endless variety of baby movements and otherworldly expressions." For him, drawing them is akin to a sensual pleasure.

Among other recurring images in Sendak's work are flying and falling figures, staples since his earliest illustrations appeared. In Ruth Krauss's *A Very Special House*, the small hero, while not actually in flight, is dancingly airborne for much of the book. In one dreamlike sequence in Krauss's *Charlotte and the White Horse*, done while the artist was still influenced by the paintings of Chagall, the heroine actually flies. Both the hero of Krauss's *I Want to Paint My Bathroom Blue* and the heroine of Doris Orgel's *Sarah's Room* are airborne for a good part of their stories, and Mickey of *In the Night Kitchen* free-falls from his bed down two floors into the Night Kitchen, a variation of flying. The hero of Jarrell's *Fly by Night* is in flight for most of his story, as is Ida, the heroine of *Outside Over There*. Whatever else it may signify, a flying figure is one that has escaped the bounds of everyday reality and clearly announces to the child viewer that the realm of fantasy has been entered. In psychoanalytic terms, a flying figure is a symbol of power and potency. Certainly dreams of flying are common in childhood.

Windows, an integral part of Sendak's imaginative life since he was a small boy, also play an important role—often a magical one—in many of his books and fantasy drawings. In Ruth Krauss's *I Want to Paint My Bathroom Blue*, they float in space with the hero. Time and again, a Sendak character will pass through a window only to be transformed into something or someone else. In *Kenny's Window*, the aperture serves as the border between the familiar reality of the boy's bedroom and both the real world beyond and the fantasy world within himself. ("A window" is the answer to one of Kenny's seven vital questions: "What looks inside and what looks outside?") A window, too, is a protection from the unknown world outside. One of Kenny's tin soldiers comments wistfully on looking through the window, "That's the world and it is miles long. We'll get lost." In *Outside Over There*, the heroine Ida's exit via a window signifies her passage from the safety and comfort of home into that unexplored dream/nightmare realm where the goblins live.

In Sendak's fantasy pages done to pieces of music, the same themes and motifs can be found—flying and falling figures, characters eating and being eaten, windows serving as passageways to other realms, and babies wailing, nursing, devouring their mothers, or being carried off. These drawings, some perfunctory in execution, others of high polish and charm, form the psychic raw material of Sendak's imaginative world.

The artist himself has often said that he has only one theme in all his work. "It's not that I have original ideas, but that I'm good at doing variations on the same idea over and over again. You can't imagine what a relief it was to discover that Henry James admitted he had only a couple of themes and that all his books were based on them. That's all an artist needs—one power-driven fantasy or obsession. And to be clever enough to do variations, like a series of variations by Mozart. They're so good that you forget they're based on a single theme."

When asked specifically what his single obsession is, Sendak has become less articulate as the years pass. "I know in my gut what it is, but it's not easy to verbalize anymore. I can't really say my theme is what children are as related to their parents, though it is certainly partly that. But it's something more as well. Whenever I get really close to it, I think 'no, it's from some deeper part of myself than my head.'"

If one were to try to verbalize Sendak's major theme on the basis of a close examination of all his books and writings, it would certainly have something to do with his unending exploration of the normal child's burden of rage, confusion, fear of and frustration with the various uncontrollable factors in his own life: adults who don't understand, limitations that restrict and inhibit, situations beyond coping with.

In his continuing attempt "to make contact with the real, underlying child," Sendak has forthrightly confronted such sensitive subject matter as childhood anger, sexuality, or the occasionally murderous impulses of raw sibling rivalry. Whenever adult critics find his work baffling or downright frightening, he is quick to point out that children are their own best censors and will neither listen to nor read on their own things that make them uncomfortable. As an author/artist of the post-Freudian world, one who has spent more time and conscious effort keeping in touch with his child-self than any previous practitioner of the art of illustration, he doubtless knows whereof he speaks.

Portrait of the Artist as a Private Person

It has often been made a subject of reproach against artists and men of letters that they are lacking in wholeness and completeness of nature. As a rule, this must necessarily be so. That very concentration of vision and inversity of purpose which is the characteristic of the artistic temperament is in itself a mode of limitation. To those who are preoccupied with the beauty of form nothing else seems of so much importance. —Oscar Wilde

Opposite: Sendak with Erda, Agamemnon, and Io. © 1976 by Nancy Crampton. Above: photograph of Sendak, about 1932

I first spoke to Maurice Sendak in the late sixties, when he telephoned me one evening because he had liked a review of mine on a book by Richard Hughes, *Gertrude's Child*. I hadn't been writing about children's books for long at that time, and to be called by someone in the field as busy and important as he already was constituted as great a professional compliment as I've ever received. We met soon after, when we were both picture-book judges for the *World Journal Tribune*'s annual Children's Spring Book Festival—a job for which Sendak had enthusiastically recommended me, I later discovered—and we have been friends ever since.

To be Maurice's friend entails both special conditions and rewards. It is not so much that he is a private person as that he is a person obsessed by his own vision of the world and the self-imposed task of communicating that vision—as purely as he is able to—in his writing and illustration. Whenever I am with him for even a few hours, he strikes me as being the most forthright and open person I have ever known. He neither shuns personal inquiry about himself nor is he shy about asking direct and searching questions of a companion. I've always felt that there is no secret I would not entrust to Maurice, and that there is nothing I could ask of him as a friend that he would not, if humanly possible, do. And yet, there is always an inhibition about intruding in his life. Just because so much of that life is inner-directed, one can never be sure where the private sector begins or ends. For example, Maurice often comes in to New York and, on more than one occasion, there has been an art exhibition in town that I know I will see and that Maurice—because of its subject matter—will also inevitably see. One such show was *Art from the World of Beatrix Potter*, which came to the Grey Art Gallery of New York University in 1977. It never occurred to me to suggest that we see it together. Somehow, I have too much respect for the uses to which he puts his time to risk imposing on it. As things turned out, we met accidentally at the show and enjoyed it thoroughly, both for its considerable merits and for the luxury of sharing insights and discoveries while viewing the works themselves.

Sendak is well aware of this distance in his relationships. In an affectionate introduction to the work of the illustrator R.O. Blechman, he wrote in 1980, "R.O. and I are typical colleague/friends. We hardly ever see each other.... This doesn't, I hope, make me less a Blechman friend. It only points up that infernal, interior insistence on work that imperiously contradicts one's normal, gregarious inclinations. Blechman understands this. My best friends in the profession are people I rarely see but whose natures and work I love."

While there may be long spaces between visits, time spent with Sendak is always enjoyable. For one thing, his enthusiasms are infectious. When he was directing the actress Tammy Grimes in the reading of *Higglety Pigglety Pop!* for his first Caedmon recording, he exhibited a small boy's pleasure on seeing his and Mozart's names linked together on a preliminary sketch for the record-album cover. "It's like a dream come true!" he said. And he is virtually irresistible when recommending a book he loves. More than once after a visit with him, I have gone directly either to my local library or to a paperback bookstore to pick up a copy of some work he has just glowingly described. Melville's *Redburn*, Charlotte Brontë's *Villette*, Dickens's *Dombey and Son*, Jules Renard's *Poil de Carotte*, and Heinrich von Kleist's *The Marquise of O* were all read in this feverish way. Sendak himself has often acted similarly on the literary enthusiasms of good friends and, as a young man, owed his introduction to Henry James, George Eliot, and others to their recommendations.

As a companion, he often delights the ear with an unexpected and absolutely on-target turn of phrase. Of a repressed and uptight fellow illustrator, he once said, "I like him despite his shortcomings, because—underneath it all—I suspect he's a closet human being." Of another colleague, whose work he finds overblown and pretentious, he noted wearily, "Oh, him again, that Charlton Heston of children's books."

The writer Doris Orgel, who has known Sendak since the mid-fifties, feels he has been one of the most influential people in her life. "I owe my entire interest in children's books to Maurice," she says. At the time they first met, through a mutual friend at the opera *Norma*, Sendak was doing the illustrations for *Seven Tales* by Hans Christian Andersen. Orgel, who was working then as a reader of adult-book manuscripts, mentioned in passing that she remembered several stories in German that had been important to her as a child growing up in Austria. "It was 1956, we were all young and gung-ho," she recalls, "and Maurice said 'Let's do them.' So I sat down and began translating a few. It's no exaggeration to say I learned to write by doing those translations. Maurice also helped me to acquire an eye for illustration, a sense of values about what to look for in pictures. And he taught me something I've never forgotten—that a picture book or longer story is nothing unless it has a fantasy element."

Sendak spent a summer vacation in the Adirondacks with the Orgels the year he was working on *Little Bear*. "He was around a lot of the time when our children were young," Doris says, "and he's entirely natural and uninhibited with kids." It was a leopard suit dearly loved and constantly worn by her son Jeremy when he was four or five, she suspects, that had something to do with Max's having a wolf costume in *Where the Wild Things Are*.

Another old friend, Roz Chertoff, characterizes Sendak as "an intense man who loves a lot of things and hates a lot of things." She remembers driving to Williamstown, Massachusetts, with him one weekend. "During the ride, he sang all of *Fidelio* in German, using different voices for the various parts. But Maurice also has a real interest in, and hunger for, popular culture," she says. "He's a TV enthusiast who watches news programs, soap operas, drama, and talk shows. And he seldom misses the rerun of a thirties film." When Mrs. Chertoff's two children were young, Sendak looked at one of the walls in their bedroom and felt it cried out for a mural. He offered to do one and then worked on it for several weeks. "It's a whole parade of Sendak characters, led off by Jennie," she says. "But Maurice never asked my kids what they'd like. It was clear from the start that this was something he wanted to do and would do in his own way. We were all delighted with what we got."

Sendak himself remarks, "I don't read to kids, I don't ask their advice and, what's more, don't ever take it when given. I just do books for them." Now that his niece and nephew, and all his friends' children, are grown up, he has very little contact with children. But he confesses to observing them all the time. "I watch them surreptitiously on the subways, or in the streets. I do my research that way."

Fabio Coen, the editor at Pantheon who commissioned Sendak to do the illustrations for Tolstoy's *Nikolenka's Childhood*, recalls how impressed he was, in the early sixties, by Sendak's dedication and commitment. "He is a man for whom no detail is unimportant," he says. "He suffered a good deal over that book, as he does over each of his books, but it never shows in the published work. I had wanted him for the Tolstoy," Coen recalls, "because of his particular feeling for nineteenth-century works. To me, *he* is a nineteenth-century artist, but one who has been affected by psychoanalysis and the pervading psychological awareness of our day."

Sendak's generosity to his various students and younger colleagues in children's books is widely known. He taught a course in children's literature at Yale for two years and, with Jane Byers Bierhorst, the children's book designer, conducted a seminar in the illustration of picture books at the Parsons School of Design during most of the seventies. "It's difficult being a teacher," Sendak says. "I never wanted to influence my students, just help to give them direction. When you have a talented kid in a class, it's tough. Part of you delights in it and another part— because you're only human, and not Dr. Albert Schweitzer—is envious." Feelings of rivalry notwithstanding, he has encouraged several of his pupils from both schools—among them Richard Egielski, Ruth Bowen, Melissa Green, Eve Rice, Airdrie Amtmann, and Paul Zelinski—to find publishers.

In the classroom, his manner was relaxed and informal, with an uninhibited give and take between teacher and pupils. One morning, when a student mentioned a handsomely illustrated version of "Snow White," which he found admirable, Sendak took exception. "That prince and Snow White are antiseptic, completely bloodless," he said. "If they get to play Parcheesi on their wedding night, it'll be a lot. And they're going to spend the rest of their lives doing greeting cards together," he said as a clincher. Occasionally, a fierce, angry side of Sendak emerges, impatient both with work and prevailing attitudes about children's books that he deplores. But if he can be intolerant and uncharitable about his colleagues in the field, he has always been extremely gentle and generous about student work. "I don't really care about seeing finished art," he told them, "I just want to know you're moving and developing." To those in his classes who were eager to achieve a recognizable style quickly, he always cautioned, "Don't be in a rush to

Opposite: record-album cover for Tammy Grimes's reading of Kenny's Window. *1977. Pen-and-ink line and watercolor. 10½ x 10¼"*

Overleaf: theatrical poster for Stages. *1978. Pen-and-ink line and tempera. 28⅛ x 14¼"*

255

skip the beginning phase. You really have to put in an apprenticeship to find out who you are." Despite his antipathy to formal education, Sendak readily admits that a stubborn resistance to formal training at the start of his own career proved costly. "I'm convinced that the surface quality of my work matured so slowly because of my inner recoil from learning from others, this complete temperamental and psychic tune-out of mine from all schooling."

Although he has become increasingly protective of his own working time in recent years, he is seldom too busy to talk with former students about their work, their aspirations, even their troubles with families when they phone him at home in Ridgefield. He has continued to make time, too, for talented young writers and artists he has encountered outside the classroom. Some years ago, a teenager named Arthur Yorinks rang Sendak's bell on West Ninth Street—where the artist had, for a long period, rented two floors of a brownstone—and left several manuscripts with him. Sendak was struck by Yorinks's originality and gift for fantasy and helped bring his later efforts to the attention of several children's book editors. Curiously, Yorinks's first picture-book text, published several years after Sendak met him, was illustrated by one of the artist's Parsons pupils, Richard Egielski. The partnership proved to be a happy one, and the two have since collaborated on two other works.

On an earlier occasion, when Sendak was autographing his books in a Village book shop, a young woman named Harriet Pincus waited to see him. Miss Pincus wanted to show Sendak some of her work. So impressed was he with her obvious talent that he later spent hours on the telephone buoying up her courage to take on a professional illustrating assignment. Sendak was as proud as a parent when her first book was published in 1967. Reviewing a later Pincus-illustrated picture book, *Tell Me a Mitzi*, Sendak wrote, "Her illustrations endow the text with the richness of a private vision, so that the book is like a glimpse into the inner workings of her own heart."

During much of the time Sendak lived at 29 West Ninth Street, he had as a near neighbor, at number 35, the poet Marianne Moore. He remembers with some embarrassment their first encounter. "One evening I got a telephone call from a woman who asked if she was speaking to the author of 'I don't care, Pierre.' 'I don't care, Pierre!,' I thought to myself and immediately suspected some sort of practical joke. I said 'yes' somewhat dubiously. 'Well, this is Marianne Moore,' the voice replied. 'And this is Ethel Merman!' I snapped back, slamming down the receiver." Some weeks later, in the Jefferson Market, Sendak recognized Marianne Moore from photographs he'd seen. Since he had long admired her work and knew she lived nearby, he went over to introduce himself. "Oh," she

Opposite: record-album cover for Gustav Mahler's Third Symphony. 1976. Pen-and-ink line and tempera. 14¼ x 14¼"

said, distantly. "You're that rude man who hung up on me when I telephoned!"

Despite the false start, they became good friends and Sendak often visited with the poet at her apartment, particularly toward the end of her life when she was ill. She, like Sendak, donated all her original manuscripts to The Philip H. and A.S.W. Rosenbach Foundation in Philadelphia where, today, there is a replica of her sitting room. In that room is a copy of Sendak's *Nutshell Library* on the table beside her favorite chair, and a drawing Sendak made for her of Puss-in-Boots hangs on the wall. Miss Moore gave Sendak a toy figure of Charlie Chaplin that she had had as a girl. "It has broken legs and is very fragile," says Sendak, "but I treasure it to this day." He also uses for his manuscripts a small leather traveling case with the poet's initials on it that had belonged to her.

Though Sendak can be scathing about children's book illustrators he dislikes, there are many colleagues whose work he admires, among them Irene Haas, Arnold Lobel, James Marshall, William Steig, Tomi Ungerer, Garth Williams, and Margot Zemach. During the fifties and sixties, Ungerer was Sendak's closest colleague/friend. The two young illustrators had first met at the Harper offices in 1956 soon after Ungerer came to this country from France. Each was about to have his own first book published, and their friendship developed quickly. Both lived in Greenwich Village, and they would often meet for coffee, or would walk together late at night, to talk about illustration, ambition, and life in general. "We were both hard workers," Sendak says, "and didn't have much time for anything but spur-of-the-moment socializing." Both their careers blossomed swiftly, but Ungerer's facile wit and polemical turn of mind led him more and more into the worlds of advertising and the political cartoon. Gradually, the two drifted apart, particularly after Ungerer left the United States in the early seventies. But, in 1975, when Daniel Keel, both Sendak's and Ungerer's German-language publisher, sent the artist an early copy of Ungerer's *Das grosse Liederbuch,* a large-format illustrated songbook for the German-language children's book market, Sendak confided, "I nearly cried at the tenderness and beauty of some of Ungerer's illustrations."

On a day-to-day basis, the artist spends a great deal of time with his three dogs; and his relationship with them—particularly with Agamemnon, the son of his female German shepherd, Erda—reveals his highly developed sense of responsibility and commitment. When Erda was two years old, Sendak decided to breed her. He spent a long time searching for a suitable male and, once Erda was pregnant, followed her progress toward confinement excitedly. He read the pertinent literature, canceled all his business engagements for the two weeks preceding the delivery date, and was present as midwife at the birth of her litter of twelve pups.

Opposite: detail of curtain design for the opera Where the Wild Things Are. *1979. Pen-and-ink line and watercolor. 7 x 9¾"*

Detail of stage-set model for the opera Where the Wild Things Are. *1979. Pen-and-ink and watercolor.*
7 x 9¾"

He was more upset than Erda when six of the puppies died, and he decided then to keep the only surviving male in the litter. Sendak never leaves for New York without stopping to say goodbye "to my boobalas" and posting detailed, individual feeding instructions for his young caretaker and gardener.

Sendak agonizes a good deal over the ups and downs of his relationship with his dogs and what influence, for bad or good, he may be having on them. Once, when he was encountering particular difficulties solving a problem in *Outside Over There*, he lashed out at Erda and frightened her badly. He was as pained as if he had let a good friend down, and he is still sensitive to Erda's occasional with-drawals; he feels sure she still remembers that black period. On his daily walks through the Connecticut woods with his dogs, Sendak is a stern master, never allowing them to run beyond the sound of his voice.

There is something akin to aesthetic pleasure in reflecting upon Sendak's life thus far. As the artist's favorite American novelist, Henry James, once said of the English painter Edward Burne-Jones, "He knew his direction and held it hard." Still a high-school student, the young Sendak confided in a school-newspaper in-terview: "I must find out more things, develop technique, and build a solid foun-dation before I can set out on an artistic career." And this is precisely what he did.

Though no one person has done more to expand the horizons of the chil-dren's picture book in our time, Sendak is without pretensions about his own talent. "My most unusual gift is that my child-self seems still to be alive and well. Of course, I can't recall the actual events of my childhood any more than most of us can; there are random scenes and sequences I remember, much as we all do. But I do seem to have the knack of recreating the emotional quality of childhood." As an English admirer, Justin Wintle, astutely observed of Sendak, "His eminence is based on a complete fusion of talent and vocation, and a sense of freshness in his work that can transform whimsy into solid fantasy." As early as the mid-sixties, the art critic Brian O'Doherty referred to Sendak as "one of the most powerful men in the United States" in that he "has given shape to the fantasies of millions of children—an awful responsibility."

Certainly Sendak the man lives a secluded and ascetic life, his days carefully ordered to eliminate unnecessary distractions so that Sendak the artist can devote himself uninterruptedly to the relentless pursuit of his mission in life. While he is working, he formally interrupts his day at about 11:00 A.M. and 4:00 P.M. to walk his three dogs, and after the late walk he takes an hour-long nap. His future projects include doing illustrations for an East European fairy tale told to him by his father just before his death. But he has also, for some time, been turning out a series of loosely-related fantasy drawings based on events in Mozart's life and mu-

Opposite: stage-set model for the opera Where the Wild Things Are. *1979. Pen-and-ink line and watercolor. 7 x 9¾"*

Left: study for the stage-set of Act I, scene iii of The Magic Flute. *1980. Pencil. 6 x 12". Right: costume sketches of Papagena and Papageno for* The Magic Flute. *1980. Pen-and-ink line and watercolor. Each 5½ x 3½"*

sic. "There may or may not be a book here," he says, "but it won't, in any event, be a work for children." More and more, Sendak is drawn to projects that link his art to music. He has written the libretto, as well as designed the sets, for the previously mentioned opera version of *Where the Wild Things Are*; provided the book and sets for a musical version of *Really Rosie*; and recently completed costumes and sets for a new Houston Opera Company production of Mozart's *The Magic Flute*. He is working, too, on costumes and sets for the Czech opera *The Cunning Little Vixen* by Janáček.

Though he has always been particularly fortunate in the ratio of his successes to his failures—even by his own strict standards—he is still always uncertain about the work in hand: "A little part of me whispers it's no good." But he is generally remarkably clear-eyed and accurate in assessing himself and others. Speaking once of a colleague who, like himself, has been highly successful, Sendak reflected, "He and I have something in common. We're both poor Brooklyn boys who've made it, and we can never quite believe this. There's always that residue of insecurity from the early days that makes us feel we'll wake up one morning, and it will all be taken away from us."

Sendak's studio in Ridgefield is at one end of his sprawling white house, and it looks out over seductive greenery on three sides—but from a safe height. Somehow, an occupant has no desire to escape from this room. In any event, it offers no exit to the outdoors. Within, the artist is surrounded by books, toys, photographs, and pictures he loves. There is a shelf full of handsomely painted, lead soldiers the artist bought in Germany; and on the walls are a large advertisement by Winsor McCay, an etching of Mozart as a young boy at the piano, original drawings by Beatrix Potter and Jean de Brunhoff, and an array of stuffed Wild Things, hand-wrought and sent to him by loving admirers over the years. Above the artist's drawing board is pinned a honeymoon photograph of his parents and a full-length picture of his paternal grandparents.

In other parts of the house are his art and book collections. There are first-rate pieces of folk art, and some handsome pieces of Early American furniture. Recently acquired are two pairs of carved wooden curtains painted in black that came off a nineteenth-century hearse. Sendak was particularly delighted because they turned out to fit perfectly the small windows in his front hall. "Here's where I'll lie in state," he says lugubriously. As befits a man of wildly contrasting tastes—the novels of Henry James and television soap operas—Sendak's house boasts both a highly sophisticated burglar-alarm system and a Mickey Mouse night-light.

He has long ago resigned himself to the fact that his books are not, and never will be, universally popular. Some years ago, he wrote in *Publishers Weekly*, "I believe

Opposite: the artist in his Ridgefield studio. © 1976 by Nancy Crampton

"New Year's Baby," for the Op-Ed page of The New York Times. *January 1, 1977. Pen-and-ink line. 10 x 7"*

there exists a quiet, but highly effective, adult censorship of subjects that are supposedly too frightening, or morbid, or simply not sufficiently optimistic for boys and girls. This should be of little importance to the creative artist whose prime concern is exploring the riches of his own remembered childhood and presenting them transmuted into artistic form for children. The artist can have—and should have—no hope of satisfying the so-called mass audience."

"All my life," he says somewhat incredulously, "I have been in the fortunate position of doing—creating—what came naturally to me. What could be more wonderful than a dream of childhood coming true? As a small boy, I pasted and clipped my bits of books together and hoped only for a life that would allow me to earn my bread by making books. And here I am all grown up—still staying home, pasting and clipping bits of books together."

A Chronology of Books

ATOMICS FOR THE MILLIONS by M.C. Eidinoff and others (McGraw Hill, 1947)

GOOD SHABBOS, EVERYBODY by Robert Garvey (United Synagogue Commission on Jewish Education, 1951)

THE WONDERFUL FARM by Marcel Aymé (Harper & Row, 1951)

A HOLE IS TO DIG by Ruth Krauss (Harper & Row, 1952)

MAGGIE ROSE: HER BIRTHDAY CHRISTMAS by Ruth Sawyer (Harper & Row, 1952)

THE GIANT STORY by Beatrice de Regnier (Harper & Row, 1953)

HURRY HOME, CANDY by Meindert DeJong (Harper & Row, 1953)

SHADRACH by Meindert DeJong (Harper & Row, 1953)

A VERY SPECIAL HOUSE by Ruth Krauss (Harper & Row, 1953)

I'LL BE YOU AND YOU BE ME by Ruth Krauss (Harper & Row, 1954)

THE MAGIC PICTURES by Marcel Aymé (Harper & Row, 1954)

MRS. PIGGLE-WIGGLE'S FARM by Betty MacDonald (J. B. Lippincott, 1954)

THE TIN FIDDLE by Edward Tripp (Henry Z. Walck, 1954)

THE WHEEL ON THE SCHOOL by Meindert DeJong (Harper & Row, 1954)

CHARLOTTE AND THE WHITE HORSE by Ruth Krauss (Harper & Row, 1955)

HAPPY HANUKAH, EVERYBODY by Hyman and Alice Chanover (United Synagogue Commission on Jewish Education, 1955)

THE LITTLE COW AND THE TURTLE by Meindert DeJong (Harper & Row, 1955)

SEVEN LITTLE STORIES ON BIG SUBJECTS by Gladys Baker Bond (The Anti-Defamation League, B'nai B'rith, 1955)

WHAT CAN YOU DO WITH A SHOE? by Beatrice de Regnier (Harper & Row, 1955)

THE HAPPY RAIN by Jack Sendak (Harper & Row, 1956)

THE HOUSE OF SIXTY FATHERS by Meindert DeJong (Harper & Row, 1956)

I WANT TO PAINT MY BATHROOM BLUE by Ruth Krauss (Harper & Row, 1956)

KENNY'S WINDOW by Maurice Sendak (Harper & Row, 1956)

THE BIRTHDAY PARTY by Ruth Krauss (Harper & Row, 1957)

CIRCUS GIRL by Jack Sendak (Harper & Row, 1957)

LITTLE BEAR by Else Holmelund Minarik (Harper & Row, 1957)

VERY FAR AWAY by Maurice Sendak (Harper & Row, 1957)

ALONG CAME A DOG by Meindert DeJong (Harper & Row, 1958)

NO FIGHTING, NO BITING! by Else Holmelund Minarik (Harper & Row, 1958)

SOMEBODY ELSE'S NUT TREE AND OTHER TALES FROM CHILDREN by Ruth Krauss (Harper & Row, 1958)

WHAT DO YOU SAY, DEAR? by Sesyle Joslin (Young Scott, 1958)

THE ACROBAT by Maurice Sendak (Privately printed, 1959)

FATHER BEAR COMES HOME by Else Holmelund Minarik (Harper & Row, 1959)

THE MOON JUMPERS by Janice May Udry (Harper & Row, 1959)

SEVEN TALES by Hans Christian Andersen (Harper & Row, 1959)

DWARF LONG-NOSE by Wilhelm Hauff, translated by Doris Orgel (Random House, 1960)

LITTLE BEAR'S FRIEND by Else Holmelund Minarik (Harper & Row, 1960)

OPEN HOUSE FOR BUTTERFLIES by Ruth Krauss (Harper & Row, 1960)

THE SIGN ON ROSIE'S DOOR by Maurice Sendak (Harper & Row, 1960)

LET'S BE ENEMIES by Janice May Udry (Harper & Row, 1961)

LITTLE BEAR'S VISIT by Else Holmelund Minarik (Harper & Row, 1961)

THE TALE OF GOCKEL, HINKEL AND GACKELIAH by Clemens Brentano, translated by Doris Orgel (Random House, 1961)

WHAT DO YOU DO, DEAR? by Sesyle Joslin (Young Scott, 1961)

THE BIG GREEN BOOK by Robert Graves (Crowell-Collier, 1962)

MR. RABBIT AND THE LOVELY PRESENT by Charlotte Zolotow (Harper & Row, 1962)

THE NUTSHELL LIBRARY by Maurice Sendak (Harper & Row, 1962): ALLIGATORS ALL AROUND, CHICKEN SOUP WITH RICE, ONE WAS JOHNNY, PIERRE

SCHOOLMASTER WHACKWELL'S WONDERFUL SONS by Clemens Brentano, translated by Doris Orgel (Random House, 1962)

THE SINGING HILL by Meindert DeJong (Harper & Row, 1962)

THE GRIFFIN AND THE MINOR CANON by Frank Stockton (Holt, Rinehart & Winston, 1963)

HOW LITTLE LORI VISITED TIMES SQUARE by Amos Vogel (Harper & Row, 1963)

NIKOLENKA'S CHILDHOOD by Leo Tolstoy (Pantheon, 1963)

SARAH'S ROOM by Doris Orgel (Harper & Row, 1963)

SHE LOVES ME, SHE LOVES ME NOT by Robert Keeshan (Harper & Row, 1963)

WHERE THE WILD THINGS ARE by Maurice Sendak (Harper & Row, 1963)

THE BAT-POET by Randall Jarrell (Macmillan, 1964)

THE BEE-MAN OF ORN by Frank Stockton (Holt, Rinehart & Winston, 1964)

PLEASANT FIELDMOUSE by Jan Wahl (Harper & Row, 1964)

THE ANIMAL FAMILY by Randall Jarrell (Pantheon, 1965)

HECTOR PROTECTOR AND AS I WENT OVER THE WATER by Maurice Sendak (Harper & Row, 1965)

LULLABIES AND NIGHT SONGS edited by William Engvick, music by Alec Wilder (Harper & Row, 1965)

ZLATEH THE GOAT AND OTHER STORIES by Isaac Bashevis Singer, translated by the author and Elizabeth Shub (Harper & Row, 1966)

THE GOLDEN KEY by George MacDonald (Farrar, Straus & Giroux, 1967)

HIGGLETY PIGGLETY POP! OR THERE MUST BE MORE TO LIFE by Maurice Sendak (Harper & Row, 1967)

POEMS FROM WILLIAM BLAKE'S "SONGS OF INNOCENCE" privately issued (The Bodley Head, London, 1967)

A KISS FOR LITTLE BEAR by Else Holmelund Minarik (Harper & Row, 1968)

THE LIGHT PRINCESS by George MacDonald (Farrar, Straus & Giroux, 1969)

IN THE NIGHT KITCHEN by Maurice Sendak (Harper & Row, 1970)

FANTASY DRAWINGS by Maurice Sendak (The Rosenbach Foundation, 1971)

THE MAGICIAN: A COUNTING BOOK by Maurice Sendak (The Rosenbach Foundation, 1971)

PICTURES BY MAURICE SENDAK (Harper & Row, 1971)

THE JUNIPER TREE AND OTHER TALES FROM GRIMM translated by Lore Segal and Randall Jarrell (Farrar, Straus & Giroux, 1973)

KING GRISLY-BEARD: A TALE FROM THE BROTHERS GRIMM translated by Edgar Taylor (Farrar, Straus & Giroux, 1973)

FORTUNIA by Mme D'Aulnay (Privately printed, 1974)

REALLY ROSIE, STARRING THE NUTSHELL KIDS scenario, lyrics and pictures by Maurice Sendak, music by Carole King, design by Jane Byers Bierhorst (Harper & Row, 1975)

FLY BY NIGHT by Randall Jarrell (Farrar, Straus & Giroux, 1976)

SEVEN LITTLE MONSTERS by Maurice Sendak (Harper & Row, 1976)

SOME SWELL PUP, OR ARE YOU SURE YOU WANT A DOG? by Maurice Sendak and Matthew Margolis (Farrar, Straus & Giroux, 1976)

OUTSIDE OVER THERE by Maurice Sendak (Harper & Row, 1981)

Index

Numbers in *italic* type refer to black-and-white illustrations. Numbers in **boldface** refer to color illustrations.

"Aladdin's Lamp" (toy), 34; **36**
Alice in Wonderland (Carroll), 206
All-American Comics, 24
Alligators All Around, 69, 71, 74, 211; **70**
Altdorfer, Albrecht, 195
Alte Pinakothek (Munich), 195
Amtmann, Airdrie, 255
Andersen, Hans Christian, 59, 61, 83, 191
Andersen, Hans Christian, Medal, 7, 17, 26, 253
Animal Family (Jarrell), 138, 144, 149; *139*
Anti-Defamation League of B'nai B'rith, 45
Arbus, Diane, 197
Ardizzone, Edward, 121, 152
Art Deco, 182
Art Moderne, 185
Art Students League, 34–35
As I Went over the Water. See Hector Protector and As I Went over the Water
Atomics for the Millions, 38; *25*
Aymé, Marcel, 35, 38, 40, 48, 51

Barnaby (comic strip), 42

Barrymore, Lionel, 23
Baruch, Dorothy, 63, 247
Bat-Poet (Jarrell), 128, 135, 149; *129*
Baum, L. Frank, 82
BBC (British Broadcasting Corporation), 151
Bee-Man of Orn (Stockton), 135, 149, 234, 239; **130–32, 133, 134**
Bergman, Ingmar, 27
Berkeley, Busby, 20, 182, 183, 185
Bettelheim, Bruno, 104
Bewick, Thomas, 151
Bierhorst, Jane Byers, 255
Blake, William, 51, 53, 138, 152–53, 185, 201
Blechman, R. O., 252
Bowen, Ruth, 255
Brahms, Johannes, *243*
Breen, Bobby, 247
Brentano, Clemens, 59, 61
Brice, Fanny, 247
Brontë, Charlotte, 252
"Brooklyn Kids, Aug. 1948" (Sendak's sketchbook), *33*
Brooklyn sketchbook, *69*
Brueghel, Pieter, 195
Brunhoff, Jean de, 269
Bumble-Ardy (film), 209
Busch, Wilhelm, 53

Caedmon Records, Inc., 252

Caldecott, Randolph, 35, 53, 110–11, 120, 135, 185, 195
Caldecott Medal, 42, 106, 107, 127, 160, 218
Canby, Henry Seidel, 64
Cantor, Eddie, 247
Carigiet, Alois, 35
CBS, Inc., 212, 227
Chagall, Marc, 24, 53, 248
Chaplin, Charlie, 260
Charlotte and the White Horse (Krauss), 53, 248; **52**
Charpentier, Gustave, 24
"Chemical Dance Floor," 38
Chertoff, Roz, 253
Chicken Soup with Rice, 69, 72, 74, 154, 210; *74*
Children of Paradise (film), 32
"Children Selecting Books in a Library" (Jarrell), 144
Christmas Mystery, 48
Chrystie, Frances, 35
Circus Girl (Jack Sendak), 50, 56; *58*, *152*
Coen, Fabio, 255
Collodi, Carlo (Carlo Lorenzini), 53
Complete Fairy Tales & Stories of Andersen, 59
Corot, Jean-Baptiste-Camille, 63
Cott, Jonathan, 13
Crane, Walter, 35, 53, 193, 197

Cruikshank, George, 35, 40, 51, 138, 193, 197
Cunning Little Vixen (Janáček), 269

Das grosse Liederbuch (Ungerer), 260
Daumier, Honoré, 35, 40
David Copperfield (Dickens), 228
Degas, Edgar, 24
DeJong, Meindert, 45, 50, 56, 127
"Devil and His Three Golden Hairs" (Brothers Grimm), 199; *199*
Devil-Doll (film), 23
Di Capua, Michael, 134, 135, 191, 192
Dickens, Charles, 17, 252
"Did You Hear What Happened to Chicken Soup?," 211; **225**
Dionne quintuplets, 235, 247
Disney, Walt, 9, 10, 19, 20, 23, 25, 26, 34, 183, 185, 209
Dodge, Mary Mapes, 82
Dombey and Son (Dickens), 252
Doré, Gustave, 40
Durell, Ann, 196
Dürer, Albrecht, 195, 197, 199, 203
Dwarf Long-Nose (Hauff), 61; *61*

"Easter Sunday, April 1949," 34
"Echoing Green" (Blake), 153
Egielski, Richard, 255, 258
Eliot, George (Mary Ann Evans), 50, 252

Engvick, William, 135

F. A. O. Schwarz, 34, 35, 40, 43
Family Circle (periodical), 48, 214
Fantasia (film), 20
Fantasy sequences, *155, 236, 237, 240, 241, 242, 243, 244, 245, 246*
Fellini, Federico, 210
Fidelio (Beethoven), 253
Fiedler, Izzy, 32; **30**
"First Schlemiel" (Singer), 140, 203
Fischer, Hans, 35
"Fisherman and His Wife" (Brothers Grimm), 191, 197, 201, 203; *205*
"Fitcher's Feathered Bird" (Brothers Grimm), 196
Fly by Night (Jarrell), 48, 215–16, 218, 229, 247, 248; *14–15, 217*
"Fool's Paradise" (Singer), 140
François, André, 51
"Frederick and His Katelizabeth" (Brothers Grimm), 195, 199
"Frog King, or Iron Henry" (Brothers Grimm), 197
Fuseli, Henry, 201, 203

Garvey, Robert, 40
Gelman, Woody, 182
Gertrude's Child (Hughes), 251
Giant Story (De Regnier), 48
Glynn, Gene, 153, 195
"Goblins" (Brothers Grimm), 140, 203, 228, 229, 247; *190*
Gold Digger series, 20
Gold Diggers of 1935 (film), 183
"Golden Bird" (Brothers Grimm), 48, 191
Golden Key (George MacDonald), 140, 145, 149, 167; *143*
Goodrich, Samuel Griswold, 157, 160, 166
Good Shabbos, Everybody, 40
Goya, Francisco de, 40
"Grandmother's Tale" (Singer), 140
Green, Melissa, 255
Greuze, Jean-Baptiste, 195
Grey Art Gallery (New York University), 252
Griffin and the Minor Canon (Stockton), 79, 82, 83, 135; *78*
Grimes, Tammy, 252
Grimm, Jacob, 191, 193
Grimm, Ludwig, 193, 197, 200, 201; engravings by, *199, 204*
Grimm, Wilhelm, 191, 193

Grimm Museum (Kassel, West Germany), 193, 195
"Grimm Reise" (Sendak's notebook), 194; *194*
Grimms' fairy tales, 40, 134–35, 140, 191–201, 203–7, 209, 214, 215, 228, 229, 235, 239
Groth, John, 35, 40
Grünewald, Matthias, 195, 203

Haas, Irene, 260
Hans Brinker, or the Silver Skates (Dodge), 82
"Hansel and Gretel," 191, 196, 201, 206; *204*
"Hansel and Gretel" (toy), 34; **39**
"Hans My Hedgehog" (Brothers Grimm), 196, 199
Happy Hanukah, Everybody, 43
"Happy Prince" (Wilde), 24
Hardy, Oliver, 179, 182
Harte, Bret, 24
Hauff, Wilhelm, 61
Haugaard, Erik C., 59
Haviland, Virginia, 17
Hector Protector and As I Went over the Water, 50, 111, 117, 120, 135, 149, 154, 163, 185, 238, 239; *113, 114–15, 117, 121, 124;* **108, 109, 112, 113, 116, 118–19, 122–23**
Higglety Pigglety Pop! or There Must Be More to Life, 17, 50, 154, 156, 160, 166–67, 171, 185, 203, 238, 239, 252; *150, 151, 158, 159, 161, 162, 163, 164–65, 168–69, 170*
Hirschman, Susan, 104
Hoban, Lillian, 29, 32
Hoban, Russell, 29, 32
Hoffmann, Felix, 35
Hoffmann, Heinrich, 53
Hole Is to Dig (Krauss), 40, 42–43, 48, 77, 210; *29, 44, 45*
Homer, Winslow, 63
Horn Book Magazine, 43
House of Sixty Fathers (DeJong), 56; *47*
Houston Opera Company, 269
How Little Lori Visited Times Square (Vogel), 77, 79; *80*
Hughes, Arthur, 53, 167
Hughes, Richard, 251
Hülsenbeck Children (Runge), 234
Hurry Home, Candy (DeJong), 45

I'll Be You and You Be Me (Krauss), 45, 124

Indolence (Greuze), 195
In the Night Kitchen, 9, 10, 17, 19, 48, 145, 149, 173–75, 178–79, 182–83, 185, 189, 227, 228, 238, 247, 248; *178, 179; 172, 173, 176, 177, 180–81, 184, 186–87, 188*
Isenheim Altarpiece (Grünewald), 195
I Want to Paint My Bathroom Blue (Krauss) 48, 248; **49**

James, Henry, 109, 248, 252, 265, 269
Janáček, Leos, 269
Jarrell, Randall, 48, 128, 134, 135, 138, 144, 149, 191, 215, 232, 247, 248
Johnson, Crockett, 42
Joslin, Sesyle, 55, 56
Juniper Tree, 40, 48, 192, 195, 197, 200, 203, 206–7, 213, 215, 228, 239; *190, 191, 198, 199, 200, 202, 204, 205*

Kafka, Franz, 216
Karchawer, Pearl, 12
Keel, Anna, 194–95
Keel, Daniel, 194–95, 218, 260
Keeshan, Robert, 77
Kenny's Window, 17, 48, 63–66, 68, 69, 75, 85, 175, 237, 248; *64;* record-album cover for, **254**
Kid Millions (film), 247
Kinder- und Hausmärchen (Brothers Grimm), 191, 193, 206, 207; *199, 204*
King, Carole, 210, 212
"King Grisly-Beard" (Brothers Grimm), 214; **226**
King Kong (film), 20, 88, 185
Kiss for Little Bear (Minarik), 144; *146, 147*
Kleist, Heinrich von, 252
Kneitel, Kenny, 182
Kollwitz, Kaethe, 24
Krauss, Ruth, 40, 42–43, 45, 48, 50, 53, 77, 79, 124, 247, 248

Ladies' Home Journal, 104
Lady or the Tiger? (Stockton), 82
Lafayette News, 24
Laurel and Hardy, 20, 179
Leonardo da Vinci, 51
Life (periodical), 104
Light Princess (George MacDonald), 55, 145, 167, 239; *148*
Lindbergh kidnapping, 235, 247
Lionni, Leo, 51
Little Bear (Minarik), 51, 53, 55, 77, 127, 144–45, 253; *55*

Little Bear's Friend (Minarik), 55
Little Bear's Visit (Minarik), 56, 144; **54**
"Little Miss Muffet" (toy), 34; **39**
Little Nemo in Slumberland (comic strip), 175
Little Passion (Dürer), 195, 197, 203
"Little Red Riding Hood" (toy), 34; **36**, (pop-up) **37**
Little Stories on Big Subjects, 45
Lobel, Arnold, 260
Louise (Charpentier), 24
Louvre Museum (Paris), 51
Luck of Roaring Camp (Harte), 24
Lullabies and Night Songs, 135, 138, 149; **5, 126, 136–37**

MacDonald, Betty, 154
MacDonald, George, 55, 140, 145, 167, 206, 239
Maggie Rose: Her Birthday Christmas (Sawyer), 40
Magic Flute (Mozart), 229, 269; *266;* **267**
Magic Pictures (Aymé), 48, 51
Mahler, Gustav, 193, 229
Margolis, Matthew, 213, 214
Marquise of O (Von Kleist), 252
Marshall, James, 260
"Master Thief" (Brothers Grimm), 201
Matisse, Henri, 24
McCay, Winsor, 53, 175, 269
McElderry, Margaret, 35
Meggendorfer, Lothar, 175
Melville, Herman, 185, 193, 252
Metropolitan Museum of Art (New York, N.Y.), 24, 175
MGM (Metro-Goldwyn-Mayer), 50
Mickey Mouse, 9, 10, 19, 25, 182, 183, 185, 269; **8, 9**
Mill on the Floss (Eliot), 50
Minarik, Else Holmelund, 51, 53, 55, 77, 144
"Mixed-Up Feet of the Silly Bridegroom" (Singer), 140
Monjo, Ferdinand, 71
Monvel, Louis Maurice Boutet de, 51
Moon Jumpers (Udry), 59, 93; **57**
Moore, Marianne, 258, 260
Moore, Noel, 154
Mordvinoff, Nicolas, 42, 48
Mother Goose, 111, 117, 120, 138, 160, 163, 166, 173; *174–75*
Mozart, Wolfgang Amadeus, 193, 229, 248, 252, 269
Mr. Rabbit and the Lovely Present (Zolotow), 61; **62**

Mrs. Piggle-Wiggle's Farm (Betty Mac-Donald), 154; *152*
Museum of Modern Art (New York, N.Y.), 24
Mussino, Attilio, 53
Mutt and Jeff (comic strip), 24
Mystery of the Wax Museum (film), 23

Narrative of Arthur Gordon Pym (Poe), 79
Nash, Ogden, 50
Nell, Richard, 34
New York Times, 43, 247; illustration for, *270*
New York Times Book Review, 218
Nicholson, William, 85
Nikolenka's Childhood (Tolstoy), 79, 82, 192, 255
Nordstrom, Ursula, 35, 38, 40, 42, 43, 48, 59, 64, 69, 71, 92, 106, 144, 232, 235
Nothing but Trouble (film), 179
Nutshell Library, 50, 69, 71, 74, 75, 77, 82, 85, 134, 189, 210, 211, 237, 260; *72, 74;* **70, 71, 73**

O'Doherty, Brian, 265
"Old Mother Hubbard" (toy), 34; **39**
One Little Boy (Baruch), 63, 247
One Was Johnny, 69, 72, 154, 237; *72*
Orgel, Doris, 59, 61, 79, 134, 248, 253
Outside Over There, 227–29, 232, 234–35, 247, 248, 265; *208, 209, 230–31, 233, 234*

Palmer, Samuel, 53, 138
Parsons School of Design (New York, N.Y.), 125, 255, 258
Perles, Ida, 72, 235
Peter and the Wolf (Prokofiev), 24
Phantom of the Opera (film), 23
Phelps, Robert, 104
Picasso, Pablo, 69
Pictures by Maurice Sendak, 167; *156* (in limited edition only)
Pierre, 50, 69, 72, 74, 82, 238; *74;* **71**
Pincus, Harriet, 258
Pinky Carrd (comic strip), 24; *24*
Pinocchio (Collodi), 53
Pinocchio (film), 20
"Pinocchio" (toy), 34; **39**
Pinocchio in Africa (Cherubini), 22
Pinwell, George, 167
Pirate Twins (Nicholson), 85
Pleasant Fieldmouse (Wahl), 127–28, 149; *127, 128*
Poe, Edgar Allan, 79

Poil de Carotte (Renard), 16, 252
"Poor Miller's Boy and the Cat" (Brothers Grimm), 199; *191*
Potter, Beatrix, 128, 154, 252, 269
Prince and the Pauper (Twain), 19, 193, 237
Prokofiev, Sergei, 24

"Rabbit's Bride" (Brothers Grimm), 196, 201; *202*
Radio City Music Hall (New York, N.Y.), 20
Rand, Paul, 51
Randall Jarrell 1914–1965, 6
Raphael (Raffaello Sanzio), 51
"Rapunzel" (Brothers Grimm), 196, 204
Really Rosie, starring the Nutshell Kids (film), 210–12, 213, 227, 269; **2–3, 21, 220, 221–24, 225**
Record-album covers, **254, 259**
Redburn (Melville), 193, 252
Regnier, Beatrice de, 45, 48, 79
Rembrandt van Rijn, 195
Renard, Jules, 16, 252
Rice, Eve, 255
Riss, Sheldon, 209, 210, 212
Rolling Stone (periodical), 13, 189
Rosenbach Foundation (Philadelphia), 260
Rossini, Gioacchino, 193
Rowlandson, Thomas, 51, 135, 138
Ruchlis, Hyman, 38
Runge, Phillip Otto, 232

St. Nicholas, (periodical), 82
Sarah's Room (Orgel), 79, 80, 248; *83*
Sawyer, Ruth, 40
Schiller, Justin, 193
Schoolmaster Whackwell's Wonderful Sons (Brentano), 61; *46*
Scott, William, 59
Segal, Lore, 191, 192
Self-portrait (1945), **33**
Self-portrait (1978), **8**
Self-portrait with Towel Headdress, **33**
Sendak, Jack, 10, 13, 17, 20, 23, 34, 50, 56, 144, 216; *11, 18, 31, 32;* **30**
Sendak, Natalie, 10, 13, 17, 19, 20, 23, 25, 34, 69, 216, 235, 237; *11, 18, 31*
Sendak, Philip, 10, 12–13, 17, 18, 23, 26, 82, 183, 216, 265; *31, 32*
Sendak, Sarah, 10, 12, 18–19, 22, 26, 152, 153, 160, 183, 216, 235; *11, 14, 18, 32;* **30**
Sendak family; 13; *10, 11*

"Sesame Street," 209
Seurat, Georges, 56
Seven Little Monsters, 218
Seven Monsters (film), 209
Seven Tales (Andersen), 59, 61, 83, 191, 253; **60**
Shadrach (DeJong), 45, 50
She Loves Me, She Loves Me Not (Keeshan), 77; *79*
Sign on Rosie's Door, 12, 68–69, 75, 85, 210, 211; *68, 69;* **67**
Singer, Isaac Bashevis, 138, 140, 149, 192
Singing Hill (DeJong), 50
"Snow White and the Seven Dwarfs," 191, 200–201, 204, 206, 255; *200*
Snow White and the Seven Dwarfs (film), 20, 23
"Snow White and the Seven Dwarfs" (models for store window), 29
Some Swell Pup, or Are You Sure You Want a Dog?, 213–15, 218, 229; **219**
Songs of Innocence (Blake), 152
Stages, poster for, **256–57**
Steig, William, 260
Sterling and Francine Clark Art Institute (Williamstown, Mass.), 63
Stevenson, Robert Louis, 138
Stockton, Frank, 79, 82, 83, 135
Story boards, 50; *213*
"Story of One Who Set Out to Study Fear" (Brothers Grimm), 195
Studio (periodical), 207

Tale of Gockel, Hinkel and Gackeliah (Brentano), 59
Tale of Peter Rabbit (Potter), 154
Taylor, Judy, 151, 152
Tehon, Atha, 138
Tell Me a Mitzi (Pincus), 258
Temple, Shirley, 247
Tenniel, John, 56
They Were Inseparable, 13
"Three Feathers," 199; *198*
Thurber, James, 138
Timely Service, 29, 32
Titian (Tiziano Vecellio), 51
Toby Tyler, 22
Tolstoy, Leo, 79, 82, 192, 255
Toulouse-Lautrec, Henri de, 211
Tray, painted metal, **41**
Twain, Mark (Samuel Langhorne Clemens), 19
"Two Journeymen" (Brothers Grimm), 203
Two Reds (Mordvinoff), 48

Ubbelohde, Otto, 197
Udry, Janice May, 59, 93
Ungerer, Tomi, 93, 121, 124, 152, 260
United Synagogue Commission on Jewish Education, 40, 43
Updike, John, 218

Verdi, Giuseppe, 193
Very Far Away, 10, 17, 66, 69, 75, 85
Very Far Away (film), 212; *213*
Very Special House (Krauss), 45, 50, 79, 210, 247
Victoria (Queen of England), 117, 120, 154, 167
Viehmann, Katherina, 193, 199; *199*
Villette (Brontë), 252
Vogel, Amos, 79
Vogel, Hermann, 195

Wagner, Richard, 120
Wahl, Jan, 127–28, 149
Weinstock, Herbert, 193
Weisgard, Leonard, 40
Weston Woods Studios, 212
What Can You Do with a Shoe? (De Regnier), 45, 79, 210
What Do You Do, Dear? (Joslin), 56, 154; *56*
What Do You Say, Dear? (Joslin), 55, 56, 59, 154; *153*
Wheel on the School (DeJong), 45, 50
Where the Wild Things Are, 7, 10, 48, 59, 72, 85, 87–89, 92–93, 96, 104, 106–7, 127, 154, 175, 185, 189, 227, 228, 238, 239, 247, 253, 269; *77, 89;* **76, 81, 84, 86, 90–91, 94–95, 97, 99–102, 105, 261, 262–63, 264**
Where the Wild Things Are (opera), 269; **261, 262–63, 264**
Whistler, James McNeill, 145
Wilde, Oscar, 24, 251
Wilder, Alec, 135
Williams, Garth, 260
Wintle, Justin, 265
Wonderful Farm (Aymé), 35, 38, 40, 48, 51
Wood, Grant, 216
World Journal Tribune, 251

Yorinks, Arthur, 258

Zelinski, Paul, 255
Zlateh the Goat and Other Stories (Singer), 138, 140, 149, 167, 192, 203, 239; *141, 142*
Zolotow, Charlotte, 61

Illustration Credits

Cover: from *Where the Wild Things Are* by Maurice Sendak, copyright © 1963 by Maurice Sendak, courtesy of Harper & Row, Publishers, Inc. and in the United Kingdom and the British Commonwealth, The Bodley Head.

Pages 2-3: from the animated film *Really Rosie, starring the Nutshell Kids*, copyright © 1976 by Maurice Sendak.

Page 5: from *Lullabies and Night Songs*, edited by William Engvick, music written by Alec Wilder, pictures copyright © 1965 by Maurice Sendak, courtesy of Harper & Row, Publishers, Inc. and in the United Kingdom and the British Commonwealth, The Bodley Head.

Page 6: from *Randall Jarrell 1914-1965*, edited by R. Lowell and others, pictures copyright © 1967 by Maurice Sendak, reprinted by permission of Farrar, Straus & Giroux, Inc. (Noonday Press).

Page 8: self-portrait by Maurice Sendak reprinted with permission from *TV Guide®* Magazine, copyright © 1978 by Triangle Publications, Inc., Radnor, Pennsylvania. Publisher wishes to thank Walt Disney Productions, Inc. for permission to reproduce Mr. Sendak's versions of Mickey Mouse on pages 8 and 9.

Pages 14-15: from *Fly by Night* by Randall Jarrell, pictures copyright © 1976 by Maurice Sendak, reprinted by permission of Farrar, Straus & Giroux, Inc. and in the United Kingdom and the British Commonwealth, The Bodley Head.

Page 21: from *Really Rosie, starring the Nutshell Kids* by Maurice Sendak, copyright © 1975 by Maurice Sendak, courtesy of Harper & Row, Publishers, Inc.

Page 25: from *Atomics for the Millions* by M. C. Eidinoff and Heyman Ruchlis, copyright © 1947, by McGraw-Hill Book Company.

Pages 29, 44, and 45: from *A Hole Is to Dig* by Ruth Krauss, copyright, 1952, as to pictures, by Maurice Sendak, courtesy of Harper & Row, Publishers, Inc. and in the United Kingdom and the British Commonwealth, The Bodley Head.

Page 46: from *Schoolmaster Whackwell's Wonderful Sons* by Clemens Brentano, translated by Doris Orgel, pictures copyright © 1962 by Maurice Sendak, courtesy of Random House, Inc.

Page 47: from *The House of Sixty Fathers* by Meindert DeJong, copyright © 1956 by Meindert DeJong, courtesy of Harper & Row, Publishers, Inc. and in the United Kingdom and the British Commonwealth, Lutterworth Press.

Page 49: from *I Want to Paint My Bathroom Blue* by Ruth Krauss, pictures copyright © 1956 by Maurice Sendak, courtesy of Harper & Row, Publishers, Inc.

Page 52: from *Charlotte and the White Horse* by Ruth Krauss, copyright, 1955, as to pictures, by Maurice Sendak, courtesy of Harper & Row, Publishers, Inc. and in the United Kingdom and the British Commonwealth, The Bodley Head.

Page 54: from *Little Bear's Visit* by Else Holmelund Minarik, pictures copyright © 1961 by Maurice Sendak, courtesy of Harper & Row, Publishers, Inc. and in the United Kingdom and the British Commonwealth, World's Work Ltd.

Page 55 (right): from *Little Bear* by Else Holmelund Minarik, pictures copyright © 1957 by Maurice Sendak, courtesy of Harper & Row, Publishers, Inc. and in the United Kingdom and the British Commonwealth, World's Work Ltd.

Page 56: from *What Do You Do, Dear?* by Sesyle Joslin, pictures copyright © 1961 by Maurice Sendak, courtesy of Addison-Wesley Publishing Company (Young Scott) and in the United Kingdom and the British Commonwealth, Faber and Faber Ltd.

Page 57: from *The Moon Jumpers* by Janice May Udry, pictures copyright © 1959 by Maurice Sendak, courtesy of Harper & Row, Publishers, Inc. and in the United Kingdom and the British Commonwealth, The Bodley Head.

Page 58: from *Circus Girl* by Jack Sendak, pictures copyright © 1957 by Maurice Sendak.

Page 60: from *Seven Tales* by Hans Christian Andersen, translated by Eva Le Gallienne, pictures copyright © 1959 by Maurice Sendak, courtesy of Harper & Row, Inc. and World's Work Ltd.

Page 61: from *Dwarf Long-Nose* by Wilhelm Hauff, translated by Doris Orgel, pictures copyright © 1960 by Maurice Sendak, courtesy of Random House, Inc. and in the United Kingdom and the British Commonwealth, The Bodley Head.

Page 62: from *Mr. Rabbit and the Lovely Present* by Charlotte Zolotow, pictures copyright © 1962 by Maurice Sendak, courtesy of Harper & Row, Publishers, Inc. and in the United Kingdom and the British Commonwealth, The Bodley Head.

Page 64: from *Kenny's Window* by Maurice Sendak, copyright © 1956 by Maurice Sendak, courtesy of Harper & Row, Publishers, Inc.

Page 72: from *One Was Johnny (The*

Acknowledgments

My special thanks go to Ursula Nordstrom, Ward Botsford, Rosalind Chertoff, Fabio Coen, Michael di Capua, Ann Durell, Susan Carr Hirschman, Ruth Krauss, Doris Orgel, Judy Taylor, and Atha Tehon for talking with me and sharing insights and recollections; the Philip H. and A.S.W. Rosenbach Foundation, Philadelphia, for cooperation in making available original drawings, sketches, and other documentary material; the staffs of the Children's Rooms of the Carnegie Library, Pittsburgh, and of the Donnell Library Center of the New York Public Library, New York City, for their help in locating crucial picture books at crucial moments; Saul Braun, Jonathan Cott, Virginia Haviland, Nat Hentoff, Walter Lorraine, and Justin Wintle, whose published interviews with the artist provided a valuable checklist of much of the subject matter to be covered; Robert Morton, Peg Parkinson, and Edith Whiteman for their editorial contributions; Joseph and Madalon Amenta, Marianne Goodman, Jack Gordon, Judith and Sheldon Gordon, Ruth Kaplan, and Lillian Whiteman for their unwavering support; Eugene Glynn for his perceptive and gently–worded critique of the manuscript when it was in a still malleable state; and to Maurice Sendak himself for his generous collaboration, faith, good humor, patience, and understanding.

S.G.L.